FUZZY-LOGIC-BASED PROGRAMMING

Advances in Fuzzy Systems — Applications and Theory   Vol. 15

FUZZY-LOGIC-BASED PROGRAMMING

Chin-Liang Chang

Nicesoft Corp., USA

 **World Scientific**
Singapore • New Jersey • London • Hong Kong

Published by

World Scientific Publishing Co. Pte. Ltd.

P O Box 128, Farrer Road, Singapore 912805

USA office: Suite 1B, 1060 Main Street, River Edge, NJ 07661

UK office: 57 Shelton Street, Covent Garden, London WC2H 9HE

British Library Cataloguing-in-Publication Data
A catalogue record for this book is available from the British Library.

ISBN 981-02-3070-2

This book is printed on acid-free paper.

Printed in Singapore by Uto-Print

Table of Contents

PREFACE

Fuzzy Logic was invented by Professor Lotfi A. Zadeh of the University of California at Berkeley in 1965. For the first 20 years, most engineers in the world paid little attention to this technology. However, since 1985, Japan has developed fuzzy logic fever, applying it to thousands of products ranging from auto-focus cameras to subway control systems. Today, fuzzy logic is used around the world in many application areas such as control, instrumentation, laboratory automation, factory automation, system identification, system modeling, pattern recognition, image database, decision support, data mining, stock selection, house hunting, investing, market survey, economic study, quality management, political analysis, insurance, resource management, and much much more ...

The purpose of this book is to introduce a Windows-based software tool for engineers and developers and to show how to use fuzzy logic in their applications. The tool is based on the programming language NICEL from Nicesoft Corporation. The approach is easy to follow: A fuzzy program is written in NICEL, which is then compiled by the tool into a subroutine in a target language. The subroutine can be called in the main program or other subroutines written in the target language.

This book will cover the programming language NICEL, and will discuss many applications that are excellent areas to apply fuzzy logic. Since the goal of this book is to develop real world applications, some reasonably-priced commercial software tools that may use subroutines powered by the fuzzy logic engine will also be described.

Because of the wide availability of personal computers, the discussion of tools in this book will be oriented toward Windows-based PC platforms. However, after learning fuzzy logic techniques, they can also be applied to applications on different platforms. For example, fuzzy logic can be used for decision support of a data warehouse on a mainframe computer, or for appliance control on a microcontroller or a special fuzzy logic chip. It is much easier to use a PC platform to build a prototype or to set up a laboratory experiment for your application, and then port it to an embedded miniature platform such as PC/104, or to a microcontroller.

ACKNOWLEDGMENTS

I would like to thank everyone who helped to see this book to completion. In particular, I would like to thank my daughter, Anna, for carefully proof-reading the manuscript, and my wife, Helen, for her support during the writing of this book. Of course, I would like to thank Professor Lotfi A. Zadeh of the University of California at Berkeley, who taught me fuzzy logic in 1965. Finally, I would like to thank Dr. Mark Liao and Dr. Jan-Ming Ho of Academia Sinica in Taiwan for expressing their interest and confidence in my work, and Dr. K. K. Phua, President and Editor-in-Chief of World Scientific Publishing Company, for inviting me to write this book.

Chapter 1   Introduction

Most of the applications that will be discussed have the following general functional blocks:

$$\text{INPUT} \rightarrow \text{DATA ANALYSIS} \rightarrow \text{OUTPUT}$$

The INPUT functional block means to get input data at a given time. Input can be single input or multiple input. If it is a single input, a single value is obtained. If it is a multiple input, more than one value is accessed. Input data may be obtained automatically by taking some measurements of a physical system such as a machine, or by asking the user to manually enter data into a form in a database system. To measure a physical quantity, e.g., speed of a car, we use a sensor to convert it into an electrical signal which is then amplified by signal conditioning. The conditioned signal is finally digitized by a data acquisition board for a computer to process.

The DATA ANALYSIS functional block analyzes input data in order to get useful output. Depending upon applications, different analysis techniques may be used. In this book, we will describe fuzzy logic programming techniques.

The OUTPUT functional block takes output value(s) computed by the DATA ANALYSIS functional block and use them for taking actions or making decisions. Different applications may mean different decisions have to be made, either automatically or manually. For example, in a control system, a <u>control decision</u> means to set a control signal or turn on/off a switch. In pattern recognition, a <u>recognition decision</u> means to classify an input pattern into a class. In desicion support, a <u>selection decision</u> may mean to select items from an output list of ranked items.

Basic Ideas of Fuzzy Logic

Fuzzy logic was invented by Professor L. A. Zadeh in 1965. Since 1985, fuzzy-logic-based controllers have been used in more than 2000 industrial and consumer products such as light rail systems, washing machines, vacuum cleaners, camcorders, rice cookers, elevator control systems, air conditioners, automobile transmissions, anti-lock braking systems, and TV enhancement systems [Bartos 1996, Intel 1994, McNeill and Freiberger 1993, Schwartz 1990, Schwartz and Klir 1992, Self 1990, Studt 1993, Williams 1992, 1995]. Commercial applications of fuzzy logic in other areas such as speech and image processing and decision support have also been available, although it is not as wide spread as in control systems.

The idea of fuzzy logic is to allow one to specify fuzzy concepts [Zadeh 1965, 1984, 1992]. A fuzzy concept can be used to modify a noun or a verb, and therefore corresponds to an adjective or an adverb. In the real world, we often have to deal with fuzzy concepts such as "high" speed, "low" temperature, "strong" signal, "tall" person, etc. A fuzzy concept can also stand for an abstract idea (such as desirability, intention, portability, etc.) which can not be directly and easily measured by physical and objective means.

A fuzzy concept such as "highness" in "high speed" is ill-defined. In this case, the fuzzy concept "highness" is related to "speed". Given a value of speed, the value of "highness" may neither be a crisp true (represented by 1) nor a crisp false (represented by 0). The value may be a degree of truth in the interval from 0 to 1, and is defined by a membership function mapping from "speed" to the interval, as proposed in [Zadeh 1965]. A value of membership function is called a grade of membership.

Each variable such as speed has a domain. Let [m,n] denote an interval from m to n. A fuzzy set for a variable is defined by a membership function mapping from the domain of the variable to [0,1]. For example, we may set the domain of the variable "speed" to be [0,100], and define a fuzzy concept "high" by a membership function mapping from [0,100] to [0,1]. Note that we restrict ourselves to the case where fuzzy logic is applied to variables whose domains are numerical.

Figure 1-1   Triangle and trapezoid membership functions

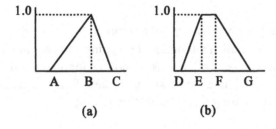

(a) A triangle membership function

(b) A trapezoid membership function

We show the two most popularly used forms of membership functions, namely triangle and trapezoid, in Figure 1-1. A triangle membership function, represented by triangle(A,B,C), is completely specified by the parameters A, B and C. Similarly, a trapezoid membership function, represented by trapezoid(D,E,F,G), is completely specified by the parameters D, E, F and G. The use of these parameterized membership functions is convenient for handling context-sensitive definitions of fuzzy concepts.

For example, different parameters can be used to define a fuzzy concept "highness" for "speed" and a different fuzzy concept "highness" for "pressure".

A fuzzy concept itself may be treated as a variable. We call it a fuzzy variable. For example, consider "safe speed", where "safeness" is a fuzzy concept and "speed" is a variable. We can treat "safeness" as a fuzzy variable, and talk about "safeness" is high, or "safeness" is low to mean, respectively, that the degree of "safety" is high, or the degree of "safety" is low. Note that the domain of a fuzzy variable is always [0,1].

Fuzzy Rules

The goal of the DATA ANALYSIS functional block in an application is to establish a functional mapping from input variables to output variables. Very often, this functional mapping is ill-defined, complicated, non-linear and uncertain. Fuzzy logic is very useful for approximating the functional mapping.

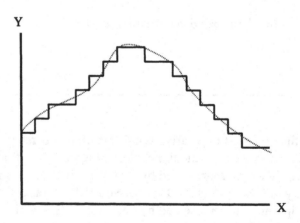

In a non-fuzzy case, the domain of each variable is quantified into a finite number of units. A functional mapping is then represented by a digitized form such as the one shown above.

In fuzzy logic, the domain of each variable is quantified into a finite number of fuzzy concepts. For example, variable "speed" may be fuzzily quantified into *low*, *medium* and *high*, and fuzzy variable "safeness" can be quantified into *low*, *medium* and *high*. A fuzzy functional mapping is then represented by a set of fuzzy rules for relationships among these fuzzy quantifications. A fuzzy rule has the form

if A1 is F1 and A2 is F2 and ... and An is Fn then B is G

where Ai is a variable or a fuzzy variable; Fi is a fuzzy quantification for the domain of Ai, i=1,...,n; B is a variable or a fuzzy variable; and G is a fuzzy quantification for the domain of B. Each "Ai is Fi", or "B is G" is called a *fuzzy literal*. The conjunction of the fuzzy literals,
A1 is F1 and A2 is F2 and ...and An is Fn,
is the *if-part*, while the fuzzy literal,
B is G,
is the *then-part* of the fuzzy rule.

An example of a set of fuzzy rules to relate the variables "speed" and "safeness" may be stated as

if speed is low then safeness is high;
if speed is medium then safeness is medium;
if speed is high then safeness is low;

where the fuzzy quantifications *low*, *medium* and *high* for the variable "speed", and the fuzzy quantifications *low*, *medium* and *high* for the fuzzy variable "safeness" are defined by membership functions.

An example of a fuzzy functional mapping between variable X and Y is shown below, where each circle or ellipse represents a fuzzy rule:

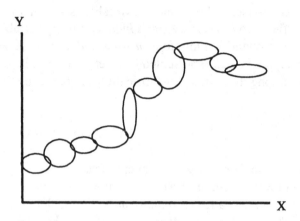

Fuzzy logic is very useful for problems where functions or relationships between variables are ill-defined, and complex. A fuzzy rule represents a fuzzy or approximate functional mapping from input variables to an output variable in a local region. Using a set of fuzzy rules, we can specify an approximate function between the input variables and the output variable for the whole interested region.

A fuzzy rule is stated in a natural language. It is straightforward, intuitive, and easy to understand.

Evaluation of fuzzy rules is carried out by performing the fuzzification and defuzzification processes. A fuzzy rule has the if-part and the then-part. Fuzzification applies to the if-part, while defuzzification to the then-part. All variables in the if-part must be bound to values in their respective domains at the beginning of fuzzification. For the if-part of the fuzzy rule,

A1 is F1 and ... and An is Fn,

fuzzification computes the strength of the if-part by evaluating the expression

$$\min \{ F1(A1), ..., Fn(An) \}$$

where min is the minimum function, and Fi(Ai) is a value of the membership function of fuzzy quantification Fi for a value in the domain of variable Ai, i=1,...,n.

For the then-part of the fuzzy rule,

B is G,

defuzzification determines a value in the domain of variable B and its weight by using the strength of the if-part and a membership function of fuzzy quantification G.

Figure 1-2 shows a pictorial representation of fuzzification and defuzzification for n=2, where x1 and x2 are values in the domains of A1 and A2, respectively. Fuzzification compares the grade of membership of F1 at x1 with the grade of membership of F2 at x2, and uses the minimum of them to cut the membership function of G. Defuzzification computes a value of B and its weight from the shaded trapezoid. There are many defuzzification methods. The singleton and centroid methods are the two most used. The singleton method takes f for the value of B, and takes m for its weight. The centroid method computes the average of B-coordinate values of the four vertices of the shaded trapezoid as the value of B, and computes the area of the shaded trapezoid as its weight.

After performing fuzzification and defuzzification for a fuzzy rule, you get a value in the domain of an output variable and a weight for the value to indicate its significance. If there are k fuzzy rules for the same output variable in the then-parts, you get k values and k weights. Taking the weighted average, you get an overall value of the output variable. When specifying membership functions of fuzzy quantifications in the then-parts, it is good practice to make sure that their sizes are approximately equal so that none of the membership functions can dominate the other by its large weight.

Figure 1-2   A pictorial representation of fuzzification and
defuzzification on a fuzzy rule

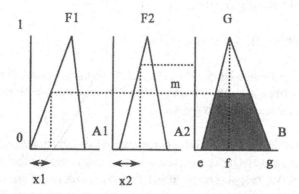

A Tutorial Example of A Fuzzy Program

In this book, we shall describe the fuzzy rule-based language
NICEL™ [Nicesoft Corporation 1994] for writing fuzzy programs
that compute values of output variables from values of input
variables. This language is based upon the ideas of fuzzy logic and
fuzzy rules that were described in the previous sections, and follows
the principles of modularization, parameterization, packaging, reuse
and a declarative (rather than procedural) approach in software
engineering and artificial intelligence. The complete language is
described in Chapter 2. An introductory example of a fuzzy program
is shown in Figure 1-3 to illustrate the main idea of the language.

Figure 1-3   A fuzzy program for computing values of fuzzy
variable "tall" from values of variable "height"

```
/* person.nl */                               /* 01 */
/*                                            /* 02 */
Copyright (c) 1994 by Nicesoft Corporation    /* 03 */
*/                                            /* 04 */

/*                                            /* 05 */
h=height;                                     /* 06 */
t=tall;                                       /* 07 */
*/                                            /* 08 */

membership pack_1(x;a,b,c,d,e,f,g)            /* 09 */
{                                             /* 10 */
 define small by trapezoid(0,0,a,b);          /* 11 */
 define medium by triangle(c,d,e);            /* 12 */
 define large by trapezoid(f,g,7,7);          /* 13 */
}                                             /* 14 */

membership pack_2(x;a,b,c,d,e,f,g)            /* 15 */
{                                             /* 16 */
 define low by trapezoid(0,0,a,b);            /* 17 */
 define medium by triangle(c,d,e);            /* 18 */
```

```
    define high by trapezoid(f,g,1,1);              /* 19 */
    }                                               /* 20 */


procedure tall(h;t; a1,b1,c1,d1,e1,f1,g1,           /* 21 */
               a2,b2,c2,d2,e2,f2,g2)                /* 22 */
    {                                               /* 23 */
    use pack_1(h;a1,b1,c1,d1,e1,f1,g1);             /* 24 */
    use pack_2(t;a2,b2,c2,d2,e2,f2,g2);             /* 25 */

    if h is small then t is low;                    /* 26 */
    if h is medium then t is medium;                /* 27 */
    if h is large then t is high;                   /* 28 */
    }                                               /* 29 */
```

In order to explain Figure 1-3, a line number has been added to each line. In general, a fuzzy program in NICEL is comprised of comment, membership package, and procedure statements. Figure 1-3 is explained as follows:

Lines 1-8 have three comment statements, each of which is enclosed by /* and */. Note that Lines 6-7 are descriptions of the variables h and t for *height* and *tall*, respectively.

Lines 9-14 show a membership package statement which defines all the fuzzy quantifications whose membership functions are shown in Figure 1-4. The membership package statement has a head (line 9) and a body (lines 10-14). The head has a membership package name and arguments consisted of a variable and parameters. The body is comprised of "define statements (lines 11-13)," each of which defines a fuzzy quantification with an optional sign of "positive" or "negative." A "define statement" is comprised of an optional sign, a fuzzy quantification and a membership function specification for the fuzzy quantification. The membership function specification has a function name and arithmetic expressions in the function arguments.

Figure 1-4   Membership functions of the fuzzy quantifications
small, *medium* and *large*

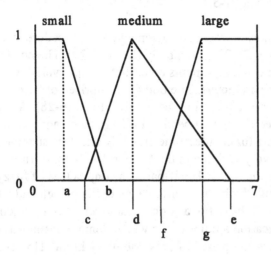

Figure 1-5   Membership functions of the fuzzy quantifications
low, *medium* and *high*

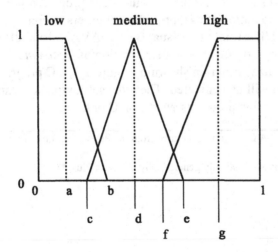

Lines 15-20 show another membership package statement which defines all the fuzzy quantifications whose membership functions are shown in Figure 1-5.

Lines 21-29 show a procedure statement. The procedure statement has a head (lines 21-22) and a body (lines 23-29). The head has a procedure name and arguments consisted of input variable h, output variable t, and parameters. The body is comprised of "use statements" (lines 24-25) and fuzzy rules (lines 26-28). A "use statement" specifies a membership package name and parameters for a variable in the fuzzy rules. One and only one "use statement" must be given for every variable in the fuzzy rules. A fuzzy rule has the if-part and the then-part. The if-part is a conjunction of fuzzy literals, each of which has a variable, an optional sign and a fuzzy quantification. If the optional sign is not given, it is assumed that the fuzzy quantification applies to the whole domain of the variable. The then-part is comprised of only one fuzzy literal. However, more than one fuzzy rule for the same variable in the then-parts can be given.

A fuzzy program is first created and then compiled into a target language. *Decision Plus*, a fuzzy-logic-based programming tool [Nicesoft Corporation 1994], provides compilers to compile fuzzy programs in NICEL into C, Visual Basic, JAVA, Visual dBase, ObjectPAL, etc. If you choose the C edition of *Decision Plus* to compile the fuzzy program shown in Figure 1-3, a C program shown in Figure 1-6 will be generated. Then, the subroutine *tall* can be used in your application programs written in C or C++.

Figure 1-6   A C program generated from the fuzzy program in Figure 1-3

```
/* PERSON.C is automatically generated by Decision Plus. */

void pack_1(
     char _fz[ ],
     char _sign[ ],
     char _mode[ ],
     char _method[ ],
     float *_weight,
     float *X,
```

```
        float * _u,
        float A,
        float B,
        float C,
        float D,
        float E,
        float F,
        float G)
{
        if (streq(_fz,"small") && streq(_sign,"whole"))
          trapezoid(_mode,_method,_weight,X,_u,0,0,A,B);
        else if (streq(_fz,"medium") && streq(_sign,"whole"))
          triangle(_mode,_method,_weight,X,_u,C,D,E);
        else if (streq(_fz,"large") && streq(_sign,"whole"))
          trapezoid(_mode,_method,_weight,X,_u,F,G,7,7);
}

void pack_2(
        char _fz[ ],
        char _sign[ ],
        char _mode[ ],
        char _method[ ],
        float * _weight,
        float *X,
        float * _u,
        float A,
        float B,
        float C,
        float D,
        float E,
        float F,
        float G)
{
        if (streq(_fz,"low") && streq(_sign,"whole"))
          trapezoid(_mode,_method,_weight,X,_u,0,0,A,B);
        else if (streq(_fz,"medium") && streq(_sign,"whole"))
          triangle(_mode,_method,_weight,X,_u,C,D,E);
        else if (streq(_fz,"high") && streq(_sign,"whole"))
          trapezoid(_mode,_method,_weight,X,_u,F,G,1,1);
}

void tall_T_1(
        char _m[ ],
        float *H,
        float *T,
```

```
      float *_w,
      float para_1[ ],
      float para_2[ ])
{
  float _u,_min,A1,B1,C1,D1,E1,F1,G1,A2,B2,C2,D2,E2,F2,G2;

  A1=para_1[0];
  B1=para_1[1];
  C1=para_1[2];
  D1=para_1[3];
  E1=para_1[4];
  F1=para_1[5];
  G1=para_1[6];
  A2=para_2[0];
  B2=para_2[1];
  C2=para_2[2];
  D2=para_2[3];
  E2=para_2[4];
  F2=para_2[5];
  G2=para_2[6];

  *_w=0;
  *T=0;
  pack_1("small","whole","fuzzify",_m,_w,H,&_min,A1,B1,C1,D1,E1,F1,G1);
  if (_min>0) {
    pack_2("low","whole","defuzzify",_m,_w,T,&_min,
  }               A2,B2,C2,D2,E2,F2,G2);
}

void tall_T_2(
      char _m[ ],
      float *H,
      float *T,
      float *_w,
      float para_1[ ],
      float para_2[ ])
{
  float _u,_min,A1,B1,C1,D1,E1,F1,G1,A2,B2,C2,D2,E2,F2,G2;

  A1=para_1[0];
  B1=para_1[1];
  C1=para_1[2];
  D1=para_1[3];
  E1=para_1[4];
  F1=para_1[5];
  G1=para_1[6];
```

```
    A2=para_2[0];
    B2=para_2[1];
    C2=para_2[2];
    D2=para_2[3];
    E2=para_2[4];
    F2=para_2[5];
    G2=para_2[6];

    * _w=0;
    *T=0;
  pack_1("medium","whole","fuzzify",_m,_w,H,&_min,A1,B1,C1,D1,E1,F1,G1);
  if (_min>0) {
    pack_2("medium","whole","defuzzify",_m,_w,T,&_min,
  }              A2,B2,C2,D2,E2,F2,G2);
}
void tall_T_3(
    char _m[ ],
    float *H,
    float *T,
    float * _w,
    float para_1[ ],
    float para_2[ ])
{
  float _u,_min,A1,B1,C1,D1,E1,F1,G1,A2,B2,C2,D2,E2,F2,G2;

  A1=para_1[0];
  B1=para_1[1];
  C1=para_1[2];
  D1=para_1[3];
  E1=para_1[4];
  F1=para_1[5];
  G1=para_1[6];
  A2=para_2[0];
  B2=para_2[1];
  C2=para_2[2];
  D2=para_2[3];
  E2=para_2[4];
  F2=para_2[5];
  G2=para_2[6];

  * _w=0;
  *T=0;
  pack_1("large","whole","fuzzify",_m,_w,H,&_min,A1,B1,C1,D1,E1,F1,G1);
  if (_min>0) {
    pack_2("high","whole","defuzzify",_m,_w,T,&_min,
```

```
                    A2,B2,C2,D2,E2,F2,G2);
  }
}

void tall(
    char _m[ ],
    float *H,
    float *T,
    float para_1[ ],
    float para_2[ ])
{
  float yy[3], ww[3];

  tall_T_1(_m,H,&yy[0],&ww[0],para_1,para_2);
  tall_T_2(_m,H,&yy[1],&ww[1],para_1,para_2);
  tall_T_3(_m,H,&yy[2],&ww[2],para_1,para_2);
  *T=average(3,yy,ww);

}
```

In the fuzzy program shown in Figure 1-3, the fuzzy quantifications for the varaible h are *small*, *medium* and *large*", and the fuzzy quantifications for the variable t are *low*, *medium* and *high*. The fuzzy quantifications for the variables h and t do not need to be different. For example, you can use the same fuzzy quantifications *small*, *medium* and *large* for variable t also. This means that the membership package "pack_1" can be shared by both variables h and t. However, the fuzzy quantifications are context-sensitive so different sets of parameters will have to be used because of the different scales for variables h and t. A different version of the fuzzy program in Figure 1-3 is shown in Figure 1-7, where r=7 for variable h and r=1 for variable t in the "use statements." When this fuzzy program is compiled, a C program shown in Figure 1-8 is generated.

Figure 1-7   A different version of the fuzzy program in Figure 1-3

```
/* person.nl */
/*

Copyright (c) 1994 by Nicesoft Corporation
*/
```

```
/*
h=height;
t=tall;
*/

membership pack_1(x;a,b,c,d,e,f,g,r)
{
 define small by trapezoid(0,0,a,b);
 define medium by triangle(c,d,e);
 define large by trapezoid(f,g,r,r);
}

procedure tall(h;t;a1,b1,c1,d1,e1,f1,g1,r1,
           a2,b2,c2,d2,e2,f2,g2,r2)
{
 use pack_1(h;a1,b1,c1,d1,e1,f1,g1,r1);
 use pack_1(t;a2,b2,c2,d2,e2,f2,g2,r2);

 if h is small then t is small;
 if h is medium then t is medium;
 if h is large then t is large;
}
```

/* Figure 1-8   A C program generated from the fuzzy program in Figure 1-7

/* PERSON.C is automatically generated by Decision Plus. */

```
void pack_1(
    char _fz[ ],
    char _sign[ ],
    char _mode[ ],
```

```
        char _method[ ],
        float *_weight,
        float *X,
        float *_u,
        float A,
        float B,
        float C,
        float D,
        float E,
        float F,
        float G,
        float R)
{
        if (streq(_fz,"small") && streq(_sign,"whole"))
          trapezoid(_mode,_method,_weight,X,_u,0,0,A,B);
        else if (streq(_fz,"medium") && streq(_sign,"whole"))
          triangle(_mode,_method,_weight,X,_u,C,D,E);
        else if (streq(_fz,"large") && streq(_sign,"whole"))
          trapezoid(_mode,_method,_weight,X,_u,F,G,R,R);
}

void tall_T_1(
        char _m[ ],
        float *H,
        float *T,
        float *_w,
        float para_1[ ],
        float para_2[ ])
{
  float _u,_min,A1,B1,C1,D1,E1,F1,G1,R1,A2,B2,C2,D2,E2,F2,G2,R2;

  A1=para_1[0];
  B1=para_1[1];
  C1=para_1[2];
  D1=para_1[3];
  E1=para_1[4];
  F1=para_1[5];
  G1=para_1[6];
  R1=para_1[7];
  A2=para_2[0];
  B2=para_2[1];
  C2=para_2[2];
  D2=para_2[3];
  E2=para_2[4];
  F2=para_2[5];
  G2=para_2[6];
```

```
   R2=para_2[7];

   *_w=0;
   *T=0;
   pack_1("small","whole","fuzzify",_m,_w,H,&_min,A1,B1,C1,D1,E1,F1,G1,R1);
   if (_min>0) {
     pack_1("small","whole","defuzzify",_m,_w,T,&_min,
     }             A2,B2,C2,D2,E2,F2,G2,R2);
}
void tall_T_2(
     char _m[ ],
     float *H,
     float *T,
     float *_w,
     float para_1[ ],
     float para_2[ ])
{
   float _u,_min,A1,B1,C1,D1,E1,F1,G1,R1,A2,B2,C2,D2,E2,F2,G2,R2;

   A1=para_1[0];
   B1=para_1[1];
   C1=para_1[2];
   D1=para_1[3];
   E1=para_1[4];
   F1=para_1[5];
   G1=para_1[6];
   R1=para_1[7];
   A2=para_2[0];
   B2=para_2[1];
   C2=para_2[2];
   D2=para_2[3];
   E2=para_2[4];
   F2=para_2[5];
   G2=para_2[6];
   R2=para_2[7];

   *_w=0;
   *T=0;

 pack_1("medium","whole","fuzzify",_m,_w,H,&_min,A1,B1,C1,D1,E1,F1,G1,R1);
   if (_min>0) {
     pack_1("medium","whole","defuzzify",_m,_w,T,&_min,
                 A2,B2,C2,D2,E2,F2,G2,R2);
   }
}
```

```
void tall_T_3(
    char _m[ ],
    float *H,
    float *T,
    float *_w,
    float para_1[ ],
    float para_2[ ])
{
  float _u,_min,A1,B1,C1,D1,E1,F1,G1,R1,A2,B2,C2,D2,E2,F2,G2,R2;

  A1=para_1[0];
  B1=para_1[1];
  C1=para_1[2];
  D1=para_1[3];
  E1=para_1[4];
  F1=para_1[5];
  G1=para_1[6];
  R1=para_1[7];
  A2=para_2[0];
  B2=para_2[1];
  C2=para_2[2];
  D2=para_2[3];
  E2=para_2[4];
  F2=para_2[5];
  G2=para_2[6];
  R2=para_2[7];
 *_w=0;
 *T=0;
 pack_1("large","whole","fuzzify",_m,_w,H,&_min,A1,B1,C1,D1,E1,F1,G1,R1);
 if (_min>0) {
  pack_1("large","whole","defuzzify",_m,_w,T,&_min,
             A2,B2,C2,D2,E2,F2,G2,R2);
  }
}

void tall(
    char _m[],
    float *H,
    float *T,
    float para_1[],
    float para_2[])
{
  float yy[3], ww[3];

  tall_T_1(_m,H,&yy[0],&ww[0],para_1,para_2);
  tall_T_2(_m,H,&yy[1],&ww[1],para_1,para_2);
```

```
tall_T_3(_m,H,&yy[2],&ww[2],para_1,para_2);
 *T=average(3,yy,ww);
}
```

References

Bartos, F.J. [1996] "Fuzzy logic reaches adulthood," *Control Engineering*, July 1996, pp. 50-56.

Intel [1994] *Fuzzy Logic Applications handbook*, Order Number 272589-002, Intel Literature Sales, P.O. Box 7641, Mt. Prospect, IL 60056-7641, USA, Tel. 800-548-4725.

McNeill, D., and Freiberger, P. [1993] *Fuzzy Logic*, Simon & Schuster, Simon & Schuster Building, Rockefeller Center, 1230 Avenue of the Americas, New York, NY 10020.

Nicesoft Corporation [1994] *Decision Plus* — A Fuzzy-Logic-Based Programming Tool, Nicesoft Corporation, 9215 Ashton Ridge, Austin, TX 78750, U.S.A., (512) 331-9027, Fax (512) 219-5837.

Schwartz, D.G., and Klir, G.J. [1992] "Fuzzy logic flowers in Japan," *IEEE Spectrum*, July 1992, pp. 32-35.

Schwartz, T.J. [1990] "Fuzzy systems in the real world," *AI Expert*, August 1990, pp. 29-36.

Self, K. [1990] "Designing with fuzzy logic," *IEEE Spectrum*, November 1990, pp. 42-44.

Studt, T. [1993] "Fuzzy logic makes products more human,"

R & D Magazine, February 1993, pp. 79-80.

Williams, T. [1992] "Fuzzy logic is anything but fuzzy," *Computer Design*, April 1992, pp. 113-127.

Williams, T. [1995] "Fuzzy, neural and genetic methods train to overcome complexity," *Computer Design*, May 1995, pp. 59-70.

Zadeh, L. A. [1965] "Fuzzy sets," *Information and Control*, Vol. 8 pages 338-353, 1965.

Zadeh, L.A. [1984] "Making computers think like people," *IEEE Spectrum*, August 1984, pp. 26-31.

Zadeh, L.A. [1992] "The calculus of fuzzy if/then rules," *AI Expert*, March 1992, pp. 23-27.

Chapter 2 The Fuzzy Rule-based Language NICEL™

NICEL [Nicesoft 1994] is designed according to the principles of modularization, parameterization, packaging, reuse and a declarative (rather than procedural) approach in Software Engineering and Artificial Intelligence. Since NICEL allows the use of fuzzy logic and fuzzy rules in an intuitive manner, software coding in NICEL is far easier and more straightforward than coding in a conventional language.

Lexical Elements

This section will cover the following different categories of tokens recognized by NICEL: Whitespace, comment, keyword, identifier, constant, operator and punctuator.

Whitespace:

Whitespace is a string of spaces (blanks), tabs and newline characters. Whitespace is used to indicate the beginning and ending of a token. NICEL is a free form language. This means that whitespace of any length can be used to improve the readability of your fuzzy program.

Comments:

A comment is a string beginning with /* and ending with */. There are restrictions on the placement of comments. Comments can not appear within other comments. A comment can only appear before and after a membership or procedure statement, or appear right after a define or use statement.

Keyword:

Keywords are reserved for special purposes and must not be used as identifier names. The NICEL keywords are:

    and
    by
    define
    if
    is
    membership
    negative
    positive
    procedure
    then
    trapezoid
    triangle
    use

Identifiers:

An identifier is a string of characters of a-z, A-Z, 0-9, and _, where the first character must be a letter a-z or A-Z. Identifiers are arbitrary names of any length given to membership packages, procedures, variables, parameters, and fuzzy quantifications. Since a fuzzy program in NICEL is compiled into a program in a target language, keywords in any specific target language must not be used as identifiers. In addition, there may be a limit on the maximum number of characters in names for variables, arrays, and procedures in a specific target language. This limit must also be observed.

Constants and Operators:

Constants are integers and real numbers. Constants and names are used with operators +, -, * and / to construct arithmetic expressions according to the following grammatical rules:

(a) A constant is an arithmetic expression;
(b) A name is an arithmetic expression;
(c) E1+E2, E1-E2, E1*E2, E1/E2 and -E1 are arithmetic expressions if E1 and E2 are arithmetic expressions;
(d) (E) is an arithmetic expression if E is an arithmetic expression;
(e) All arithmetic expressions are generated by applying the above rules.

Arithmetic expressions can appear in arguments of a membership function to be discussed later.

Arithmetic expressions are used with boolean operators $<$, $<=$, $=$, $>$, $>=$ and $><$ to construct boolean expressions. That is, if E1 and E2 are arithmetic expressions, then E1$<$E2, E1$<=$E2, E1$=$E2, E1$>$E2, E1$>=$E2 and E1$><$E2 are boolean expressions which can be used as constraints. Note that $><$ is read as "not equal to."

<u>Punctuators</u>:

The punctuators used in NICEL are

$$; , ( ) \{ \}$$

The semicolon " ; " is used to indicate the end of a "define," "use," or "if-then" statement. It is also used to separate between variables and parameters, and between input and output variables.

The comma "," separates the elements of a variable list, a parameter list, or an arithmetic expression list.

The pair of parentheses "( )" is used to group arithmetic expressions and to enclose argument lists in a membership statement, procedure statement, or membership function.

The pair of braces "{ }" is used to enclose the body of a membership or procedure statement.

Language Structure

This section is concerned with the legal ways in which tokens can be grouped together to form expressions and statements.

Domains:

A domain for a variable is all the values the variable can assume. For example, the domain of age is all positive integers from 0 to 120. In NICEL, only numerical domains are used. A numerical domain has a lower and upper limit. A membership function defined on a numerical domain must have a lower and upper limit.

Fuzzy Quantifications:

A fuzzy quantification for a variable is characterized by a membership function F mapping from the domain of the variable to the interval [0,1]. The value F(x) for a particular value x of the variable denotes the degree of the membership that x belongs to the fuzzy quantification. An identifier is used to name a fuzzy quantification. Most of the time, a fuzzy quantification name is an adjective applying to a noun. For example, speed is a noun, and has a range of values. "Low" applying to "speed" is a fuzzy quantification characterized by a membership function that specifies the degree of "low" for each value of speed. For example, if "low" is defined by the triangle membership function, triangle(0,0,30), as shown in Figure 2-1, then the degree of "low" at the speed equal to 15 is 0.5. In addition, any fuzzy concept such as "recession" or "growth" which has a degree of truth or membership can be treated as fuzzy variables. In this case, a fuzzy quantification for a fuzzy variable is a second order fuzzy concept. For example, "market strength" and "electability" are fuzzy variables. That is, values for "market strength" and "electability" are from 0 to 1. However, when we talk about *high* or *low* "market strength" and *high* or *low* "electability", the *"high"* or *"low"* here are second order fuzzy concepts. Very often, it is not easy to directly specify membership functions of "market strength" and "electability". Therefore, they are indirectly and intuitively approximated by using fuzzy rules in terms of other input variables. Through the defuzzification of the fuzzy quantifications "*high*" and "*low*" in the fuzzy rules, the degrees of "market strength" and "electability" can be computed from values of the input variables.

Figure 2-1 A membership function for low speed

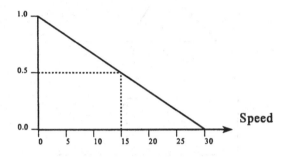

Membership Functions:

A membership function can have any shape. In this book, only the membership functions which have the triangle and trapezoid shapes are used. These two shapes are the most popular ones used in defining membership functions. Figure 2-2 shows a triangle and a trapezoid membership function. Since the vertex coordinates A, B, and C completely define the triangle membership function, it can be represented by triangle(A,B,C). Similarly, D, E, F and G completely define the trapezoid membership function, and therefore it is represented by trapezoid(D,E,F,G). The use of these parameterized membership functions is convenient for handling context-sensitive definitions of fuzzy quantifications. For example, different parameters can be used to define "small" for "height" and "small" for "tallness".

Figure 2-2   Triangle and trapezoid membership functions

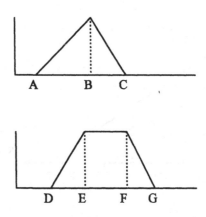

Arguments of the functions triangle and trapezoid are not just restricted to parameters. Any arithmetic expressions can be used for the arguments. This provides an easy way to specify translations, mirror images and other transformations of membership functions. Here are some examples:

triangle(a,b,c)	a membership function
triangle(-c,-b,-a)	the mirror image of triangle(a,b,c)
triangle(a-5,b-5,c-5)	a translation of triangle(a,b,c)
triangle(-2*a,0,2*a)	a widening of triangle(-a,0,a)
triangle(-0.5*a,0,0.5*a)	a narrowing of triangle(-a,0,a)
trapezoid(d,e,f,g)	a membership function
trapezoid(-g,-f,-e,-d)	the mirror image of trapezoid(d,e,f,g)
trapezoid(d+2*h,e+2*h,f+2*h,g+2*h)	a translation of trapezoid(d,e,f,g)

Transformations of membership functions are useful for specifying fuzzy hedges. For example, "very_small" and "very_very_small" are hedged on "small". Membership functions of "very_small" and "very_very_small" can be defined by transformations of a membership function of "small". Note that a fuzzy quantification name is an identifier, and therefore the underscores in "very_small" and "very_very_small" are necessary.

Define Statements:

Define statements are used to define fuzzy quantifications by parameterized membership functions. A define statement has following the form:

define [<sign>] <fuzzy_quantification>
by <membership_function> [,<constraint>,...,<constraint>];

where

<sign> is positive or negative, and is optional,
<fuzzy_quantification> is an identifier denoting
        the name of a fuzzy quantification,
<membership_function> is either triangle(A,B,C)
                or trapezoid(D,E,F,G), and
each <constraint> is a boolean expression.

Note that A,B,C,D,E,F,G in <membership_function> are arithmetic expressions.

The following are examples of define statements:

define positive small by triangle(0,0,a);
define negative medium by triangle(b,c,d), c>0;
define f1 by triangle(-1-b, 0, 1+b);

The signs "positive" and "negative" mean that a define statement is defined for positive and negative values of a variable, respectively. If no sign is given in a define statement, it means that the define statement is defined for the whole domain of values.

Membership Package Statements:

Given a variable, many fuzzy quantifications may be defined for it to indicate its various qualitative states. For example, for variable "speed", we can talk about *low* speed, *medium* speed, and *high* speed. In this case, there are 3 fuzzy quantifications: *low*, *medium*, and *high*, that are associated with "speed". It is often convenient to group the definitions of all these fuzzy quantifications in a package represented by a membership package statement shown below:

```
membership <package_name>(<var>;<para>,...,<para>)
{
    <define_statement>
             .
             .
             .
    <define_statement>
}
```

where

<package_name> is an identifier denoting a package name,
<var> is an identifier denoting a variable,
each <para> is an identifier denoting a parameter, and
each <define_statement> is a define statement.

An example of a membership package statement is shown below:

```
membership size_terms(x;a,b,c,d,e,f,g,h)
{
 define positive small by triangle(0,0,a);
 define positive medium by triangle(b,c,d), c > 0;
 define positive large by trapezoid(e,f,g,h), f > c;
 define negative small by triangle(-a,0,0);
                         /* mirror image of positive small */
 define negative medium by triangle(-d,-c,-b);
                         /* mirror image of positive medium */
 define negative large by trapezoid(-h,-g,-f,-e);
                         /* mirror image of positive large */
}
```

The membership functions in the above package are shown in Figure
2-3.

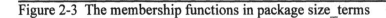

Figure 2-3 The membership functions in package size_terms

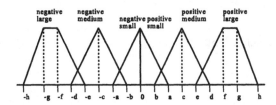

The family of the fuzzy quantifications *small*, *medium*, and *large* in the above package are related to a "quantity" type. Within the same membership package statement, different families of fuzzy quantifications related to different types can be specified, if needed. For example, *low*, *medium* and *high* speeds are related to "velocity"; and *safe* and *dangerous* speeds are related to "safety" as shown below:

```
membership package_1(speed;a,b,c,d,e,f,g,h,i,j,k)
{
  define low by triangle(0,0,a);
  define medium by triangle(b,c,d);
  define high by triangle(e,f,f);

  define safe by trapezoid(0,0,g,h);
  define dangerous by trapezoid(i,j,k,k);
}
```

The membership functions for the two families of the fuzzy quantifications in the above package are shown in Figure 2-4.

Figure 2-4   The membership functions for the two families of
               fuzzy quantifications for a single variable "speed"

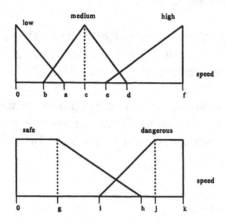

The advantage of the membership package is that it may be used for
and shared by different variables using different sets of parameters.
In addition, the mechanism of parameter passing is convenient for
experimenting with different membership functions in order to find
a good solution. If it is necessary, more than one membership
package statement may be written in a fuzzy program.

Use Statements:

A use statement specifies which membership package is used by a
variable. Its syntax is

     use <package_name>(<var>;<para>,...,<para>);

where
       <var> is an identifier denoting a variable, and
       each <para> is an identifier denoting a parameter.

It is possible for the same package to be used by more than one variable using different sets of parameters. The following are examples of use statements:

    use size_terms(speed_error;a1,b1,c1,d1,e1,f1,g1,h1);
    use size_terms(pressure_difference;a2,b2,c2,d2,e2,f2,g2,h2);
    use size_terms(temperature_deviation;a3,b3,c3,d3,e3,f3,g3,h3);

How "use statements" are specified in a procedure statement will be explained later in this chapter. Within a procedure statement, one and only one use statement must be specified for each variable.

Literals:

A literal has the form

<var> is [<sign>]/<fuzzy_quantification>/.../<fuzzy_quantification>

where
    <var> is an identifier denoting a variable,
    <sign> is positive or negative, and is optional, and
    each <fuzzy_quantification> is an identifier denoting
    a fuzzy quantification name.

Examples are:

    x is small
    y is positive/expensive/medium
    z is negative/large
    speed is high/dangerous

A "/" is interpreted as a conjunction. A simple literal is a literal containing only one fuzzy quantification. For instance, the first and third literals in the above examples are simple literals. If no sign is given in a literal such as the above first literal, the default is "whole."

If a literal contains more than one fuzzy quantification, such as the second and fourth literals in the above example, all the fuzzy quantifications in the literal must be defined in the same membership package statement. For instance, in the literal, "speed is high/dangerous," the fuzzy quantifications "high" and "dangerous" are defined in the same membership package as shown in Figure 2-4.

Fuzzy Rule Statements:

A fuzzy rule statement has the following format:

    if   <literal> and ... and <literal>
    then <literal> and ... and <literal>;

where
    each <literal> is a literal.

The *if-part* is the expression between "if" and "then," while the *then-part* is the expression between "then" and ";". The if-part and then-part are also called the left hand side (LHS) and the right hand side (RHS) of the rule, respectively. A fuzzy rule statement is also called an if-then statement.

When a fuzzy rule is analyzed, it will be decomposed into n fuzzy rules if there are n fuzzy quantifications in the right hand side of the fuzzy rule. For example, suppose f1,f2,f3,g1,g2 and h1 are fuzzy quantifications. If the following fuzzy rule is given,

    if x is positive/f1/f2/f3
    then y is positive/g1/g2 and z is h1;

then it will be decomposed into the following 3 fuzzy rules:

    if x is positive/f1/f2/f3 then y is positive/g1;
    if x is positive/f1/f2/f3 then y is positive/g2;
    if x is positive/f1/f2/f3 then z is h1;

Furthermore, the literal in the left hand side of these fuzzy rules will be normalized into the conjunction of the 3 simple literals as follows:

> if x is positive/f1 and x is positive/f2 and x is positive/f3
> then y is positive/g1;

> if x is positive/f1 and x is positive/f2 and x is positive/f3
> then y is positive/g2;

> if x is positive/f1 and x is positive/f2 and x is positive/f3
> then z is h1;

Note that a fuzzy quantification (with or without a sign) in every simple literal of a fuzzy rule must be defined in a membership package statement. For example, if
> positive small,
> negative small, and
> small
are defined for variable x, the following can respectively be used in a fuzzy rule:
> x is positive/small,
> x is negative/small, and
> x is small.

To avoid confusion and the difficulty that may be associated with defuzzification, the following literal,
> x is small,
 cannot be used even when both
> positive small, and
> negative small
are defined in a membership package statement.

Similarly, the following literal,
> x is positive/small, or
> x is negative/small,
cannot be used even when "small" is defined.

In a procedure statement containing fuzzy rules, all the fuzzy quantifications for every variable must be defined in the same membership package statement. The detail will be described later.

<u>Procedure Statements</u>:

A procedure statement has the form:

```
procedure <name> (  <in_var>,...,<in_var>;
                    <out_var>,...,<out_var>;
                    <para>,...,<para> )
{
   <use_statement>
          .
          .
          .
   <use_statement>

   <fuzzy_rule_statement>
          .
          .
   <fuzzy_rule_statement>
}
```

where
   <name> is an identifier denoting a procedure name,
   each <in_var> is an identifier denoting an input variable,
   each <out_var> is an identifier denoting an output variable,
   each <para> is an identifier denoting a parameter,
   each <use_statement> is a use statement, and
   each <fuzzy_rule_statement> is a fuzzy rule statement.

A procedure must contain at least one input variable, one output variable, two use statements and one fuzzy rule.

Within a procedure statement, one and only one use statement must be specified for each variable.

A fuzzy procedure can be easily modified. Fuzzy rules can be deleted and added to the fuzzy procedure. It can contain redundant and contradictory fuzzy rules, and still compute robust values of the output variables.

In a procedure statement, all input variables must appear in the if-parts of fuzzy rules. However, an output variable may appear in the then-part of a fuzzy rule as well as in the if-part of another fuzzy rule. In this case, there is a dependency between the fuzzy rules. To schedule the rule execution sequence, the *Decision Plus* compiler [Nicesoft 1994] will construct a dependency graph as follows:

(1) Group all the fuzzy rules in the procedure statement by variables in the then-parts of the fuzzy rules. Each group of fuzzy rules that have the same variable V in their then-parts is denoted by V. Every group is represented by a node.

(2) Draw a directed arc from node V1 to node V2 if V1 is used in the if-part of a fuzzy rule in group V2. Node V2 is called a *child node* of node V1, and node V1 is called a *parent node* of node V2.

(3) The rule execution sequence must conform to the dependency graph in such a way that no fuzzy rule in a child node is executed before a fuzzy rule in a parent node. However, fuzzy rules within a group can be executed in parallel. In order to avoid a deadlock, a dependency graph can not have cycles.

Fuzzy Programs:

A fuzzy program consists of one or more membership package statements, and one procedure statement. The membership package statements define fuzzy quantifications used in fuzzy rules of the procedure statement.

An Example of a Fuzzy Porgram

In this section, an example will be given to show how a fuzzy program can be written to solve problems. Let us consider a simple drug-delivering system that decides the dose of a drug for a patient. Assume that a dose is dependent on the patient's height, weight, and age. We also assume from an intuitive judgement that the dose depends on how big the patient is. Since "big" is a fuzzy concept, we choose it to be a fuzzy variable whose values are to be determined by fuzzy rules in terms of variables "height" and "weight." Given the size and age of the patient, the amount of the dose of drug can be determined. That is, the dose may be determined by fuzzy rules in terms of variables "bigness" and "age." A fuzzy program based upon these intuitive reasoning is shown in Figure 2-5. Note that this fuzzy program is created just for the illustration, and is not meant to be used in a real application.

Figure 2-5   A fuzzy program for computing a drug dose

```
/* dose.nl */
/*
Copyright (c) 1996 by Nicesoft Corporation
*/

/*
h=height
w=weight
age=age
b=bigness
dose=dose
*/

membership pack_1(x;a,b,c,d,e,f,g,r)
{
  define small by trapezoid(0,0,a,b);
  define medium by triangle(c,d,e);
  define large by trapezoid(f,g,r,r);
}
```

```
procedure dose(ht,wt,age;
              bg,dose;
              a1,b1,c1,d1,e1,f1,g1,r1,
              a2,b2,c2,d2,e2,f2,g2,r2,
              a3,b3,c3,d3,e3,f3,g3,r3,
              a4,b4,c4,d4,e4,f4,g4,r4,
              a5,b5,c5,d5,e5,f5,g5,r5)
{
 use pack_1(ht;a1,b1,c1,d1,e1,f1,g1,r1);
 use pack_1(wt;a2,b2,c2,d2,e2,f2,g2,r2);
 use pack_1(age;a3,b3,c3,d3,e3,f3,g3,r3);
 use pack_1(bg;a4,b4,c4,d4,e4,f4,g4,r4);
 use pack_1(dose;a5,b5,c5,d5,e5,f5,g5,r5);


 if ht is small and wt is small then bg is small;
 if ht is medium and wt is medium then bg is medium;
 if ht is large and wt is medium then bg is large;
 if wt is large then bg is large;

 if age is small then dose is small;
 if bg is small and age is medium then dose is medium;
 if bg is medium and age is medium then dose is large;
 if bg is large and age is medium then dose is large;
 if age is large then dose is medium;
}
```

Notice that this fuzzy program has two groups of fuzzy rules. The first 4 fuzzy rules compute values of the variable "bg," while the remaining fuzzy rules compute values of the variable "dose." The dependency graph shown in Figure 2-6 shows the dependencies of each variable. The dependency graph has a network structure similar to a neural net. The difference is that in a neural net, a variable is related to other variables by a composition of a step function and a linear function, while in a dependency graph of a fuzzy program, a variable is related to other variables by a set of fuzzy rules.

Figure 2-6   The dependency graph for the variables in
a fuzzy program shown in Figure 2-5

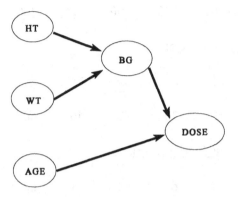

The fuzzy program shown in Figure 2-5 can be compiled into a C
program, or a program in another target language. Before calling the
procedure *dose,* parameters need to be chosen. In general, there are
no guidlines on how to select a good set of parameters except by
intuitive judgement. Initially, a set of parameters is chosen. If results
are not good, they can always be changed. In a section on **Machine
Training** in Chapter 9, there will be a discussion on how algorithms
can be used to adjust parameters automatically for a given set of
input and output data.

For this example, we may choose the following parameters:

Parameters for height (variable ht):

a1	b1	c1	d1	e1	f1	g1	r1
4	5	4	5	6	5	6	10

Parameters for weight (variable wt):

a2	b2	c2	d2	e2	f2	g2	r2
40	80	40	120	200	120	200	400

Parameters for age (variable age):

a3	32	c3	d3	e3	f3	g3	r3
10	20	10	20	60	40	60	100

Parameters for bigness (variable bg):

a4	b4	c4	d4	e4	f4	g4	r4
0.2	0.4	0.2	0.4	0.6	0.5	0.8	1.0

Parameters for dose (variable dose):

a5	b5	c5	d5	e5	f5	g5	r5
1	4	1	3	5	3	5	10

The membership functions with these parameters are show in Figure 2-7, where the domains of the variables are respectively set to 0-10 feet for height, 0-400 pounds for weight, 0-100 years for age, 0.0-1.0 degree of truth for bigness, and 0-10 units for dose

Figure 2-7   Some specific membership functions

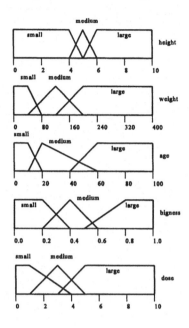

References

Nicesoft Corporation [1994] *Decision Plus* — A Fuzzy-Logic-
Based Programming Tool, Nicesoft Corporation,
9215 Ashton Ridge, Austin, TX 78750, U.S.A.,
(512) 331-9027, Fax (512) 219-5837.

Chapter 3   Data Acquisition

In application areas such as laboratory automation, process monitoring and control, electronics testing, manufacturing, automotive and aerospace engineering, medical research, and educational instruction and research, the first thing that is necessary is hardware and software that measures and acquires physical phenomena data. Because of the wide spread of personal computers (PCs), we can use PCs as platforms for data acquisition. Figure 3-1 shows a general PC-based data acquisition system. All the components in this system can be purchased from various vendors. Therefore, it is very easy to set up a PC-based data acquisition system.

Figure 3-1   A PC-based Data Acquisition System

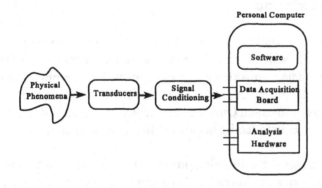

Transducers

Transducers sense physical phenomena and produce electrical signals that the data aquisition board can accept. There are all kinds of transducers and sensors. For example, a thermocouple, thermistor, or a resistive temperature detector can be used to measure temperature. To measure force, rate of flow, and pressure, a strain gauge, flow meter, and pressure tranducer, can be used respectively. There are also proximity sensors for measuring distances. In general, there are transducers and sensors for any physical, chemical (e.g., pollutant), and geometric quantities that need to be measured. Some companies that provide sensors and transducers are listed in Appendix A.

Electrical signals produced by transducers should be proportional to the physical quantities that they are measuring. However, there may be uncertainties due to the transducers' sensitivity to temperature. In addition, the transducers may behave non-linearly. More circuits can be added to compensate for the uncertainty and non-linearity, but better precision will cost more money. The advantage of using fuzzy logic is that inexpensive transducers and simple data analysis can be used and still receive good results.

Signal Conditioning

The purpose of signal conditioning hardware is to amplify and, in some cases, linearize electrical signals generated by tranducers into a form that a data acquisition board can accept. For example, low-level thermocouple signals should be amplified to increase the measurement resolution. Once an electrical signal is amplified, it is less likely to be distorted by noise on a line to a computer.

For safety, a signal conditioning product may also be used to isolate a computer from an industrial high-voltage, high-current device or a machine that is to be monitored and controlled. For example, a valve may require 100 volts AC electrical signal at 2 ampers to operate. However, a data acquisition board has only 0 to 5 volts DC at several milliamperes. Signal conditioning hardware can act as a coupler between the valve and the board.

A signal conditioning product may include a filter and an electrical excitation source. For example, a lowpass filter can be used to eliminate high frequencies, and an elctrical excitation source is required for a strain gauge to produce an electrical signal.

Data Acquisition Boards

A data acquisition board is hardware that is plugged in a PC slot. It contains circuits for analog inputs, analog outputs, digital I/O, and timing I/O. Some companies that make plug-in data acquisition boards are listed in Appendix B.

Analog Inputs

When purchasing a data acquisition board, there are many factors to consider. For analog inputs, it is important to consider the number of channels, sampling rate, resolution, and range.

Since one channel accepts one analog input, the number of analog input channels should be greater than the number of inputs that is to be measured. An analog signal is digitized by an A/D converter at a sampling rate. The higher the change rate of the signal, the higher the sampling rate is required. For example, human voice signals have frequency components up to 3 kHz. To get a good representation of the signals, the sampling rate should be at least twice the rate of the maximum frequency component. Therefore, you need a sampling rate greater than 6 kHz for the human voice signals. Audio signals from musical instruments have frequency components up to 20 kHz. In this case, you need a sampling rate greater than 40 kHz. Signals produced by temperature transducers usually do not require a high sampling rate because temperature does not change quickly in most applications. However, if noise signals are present in the temperature measurements, it is a good idea to sample temperature at a higher rate and compute an average for every 3 or 4 samples in order to eliminate noise errors.

A data aquisition board may contain a multiplexer so that a single A/D converter can be used for more than one analog input channel. That is, the input channels are connected to the A/D converter through the multiplexer so that the A/D converter can sample one channel, switch to the next channel, sample it, switch to the next channel, and so on.

Resolution is the number of bits that the A/D converter uses to represent an input signal voltage. If you use 8-bit resolution, the range of input signal values can be quantized into 256 units. If you use 16-bit resolution, it can be quantized into 65,536 units. Therefore, the higher the resolution, the smaller the detectable signal voltage change. In order to compute the actual voltage value a unit represents, we need to know the voltage range that the A/D converter is set to. A data acquisition board may have voltage ranges selectable at 0 to 10 V, 0 to 5 V, -10 to 10 V, or -5 to 5 V. With a voltage range of 0 to 5 V and a resolution of 8-bit, the actual voltage of a unit is 5/256 V. If the input singal is amplified 500 times before it is sent to the A/D converter, then the actual voltage of a unit is 5/(500*256) V. Therefore, given a board's voltage range and amplification gain, the computer can scale a binary code from the A/D converter into an actual voltage value. In applications where measuring physical quantities is more important than getting actual voltages from a transducer, the known values of the physical quantities can be used to calibrate them.

Analog Outputs

Analog output circuitry is needed to stimulate a process or unit under test in a data acquisition system. The factors that should be considered for analog outputs are resolution, settling time, and slew rate. A binary code is converted into an analog voltage by a D/A converter. The number of bits in the binary code is output resolution. The higher the resolution, the smoother the analog output voltage will be.

The settling time is the time required by the D/A converter to settle to a specific output voltage. The slew rate is the maximum rate of change that the D/A converter can produce on the output signal. Generating high-frequency signals generally requires a small settling time and a high slew rate.

Digital I/O

Digital I/O interfaces on a data acquisition board are often used to control processes, generate test patterns, and communicate with peripheral equipments. The factors that should be considered for digital I/O are the number of digital lines available, the rate at which digital data can be inputed and outputed on these lines, and the drive capability of the lines. A signal conditioning module may be required if the drive capability is not large enough for your applications.

Timing I/O

Counter/timer circuitry is used to count the occurrences of a digital event, measure digital pulse timing, and generate square wave and pulses. The factors that should be considered for timing I/O are the resolution and clock frequency of a counter. The resolution is the number of bits the counter uses to count with. The higher the resolution, the higher the counter can count. The clock frequency determines the frequency of a generated square wave.

Real-Time System Integration (RTSI)

Some vendors provide ways to synchronize operations in a data acquisition board. For example, National Instruments [National Instruments 1996] uses RTSI bus to synchronize A/D conversions, D/A conversions, digital inputs, digital outputs, and counter/timer operations. This is very useful for many applications. For example, a

RTSI bus can be used to capture several analog inputs, while simultaneously generating an output pattern synchronized to the sampling rate of the inputs.

Analysis and Interface Hardware

In applications such as speech processing and image processing, large computation power is required. Since a PC may not process speech/image signals in the time required by certain applications, it pays to have a Digital Signal Processing (DSP) hardware to perform specific mathematical operations such as fast Fourier Transform (FFT), filtering, correlation, vector multiplication and vector maximum on digitally represented signals. For example, if FFT is performed on a DSP hardware, you can gain a speed of 100:1 over the PC.

Another hardware often used with a PC is interface hardware. This connects the PC to various types of instruments. Interface hardware is needed when there are already existing instruments in your laboratory/factory, or when you want to take the advantage of the instrument's special functions and performance.

The interface bus used in an instrument can be the RS-232 port, the IEEE 488 General Purpose Interface Bus (GPIB), or the VME eXtension for Instrument (VXI) bus. Many vendors such as National Instruments supply different interface hardware for these types of instruments. When purchasing an interface card for a specific instrument, an important thing to check for is that the driver for controlling the instrument is included.

LabWindows/CVI

LabVIEW and LabWindows/CVI are software products developed by National Instruments.

LabVIEW is a graphical programming system for data acquisition and control, data analysis, and data presentation. LabVIEW offers an innovative programming methodology in which software modules called Virtual Instruments (VIs) are graphically assembled. This is similar to designing a block or data flow diagram. Because the execution order in LabVIEW is determined by the flow of data between blocks and not by sequential lines of codes, diagrams that have multiple data paths and simultaneous operations can be easily created. Consequently, LabVIEW is a multitasking system running multiple execution threads, multiple virtual instruments, and other applications.

LabWindows/CVI provides acquisition, analysis, and presentation capabilities for C programmers. The LabWindows development system has extensive libraries of functions for data acquisition, data analysis, and data presentation. LabWindows is built on top of National Instruments' instrument drivers for a variety of instrumentation hardware products.

With LabWindows, you control instrumentation and acquire data using GPIB, VXI, and RS232 instruments, and plug-in data acquisition boards. The libraries of functions in LabWindows relieve you from knowing the intricacies of programming your instruments, and you can easily analyze and display the results of your measurement and control operations.

LabWindows will be briefly covered in this section, focusing on the idea of integrating C programs generated from fuzzy-logic-based programming tools.

LabWindows provides a large collection of DAQ functions for interfacing with data acquisition boards and instruments. It also provides a rich set of Graphical User Interface (GUI) functions that can be used to present data on the computer screen. Appendix C shows the lists of the DAQ and GUI functions. Detailed descriptions of these functions are given in National Instruments' INSTRUPEDIA [National Instruments 1996] on a CD-ROM, which is available free upon request.

In the following, we give a tutorial example to illustrate on how to write a C program that call LabWindows functions, and other C programs generated from fuzzy-logic-based programming tools. Note that the approach described here is applicable for the users of LabWindows as well as other programming tools such as ComputerBoards' UniversalLibrary in Appendix D.

Consider a simple control problem: Every morning, the outdoor air temperature and soil moisture are measured. The problem is to decide how long a sprinkler should be turned on. An experimental setup is shown below:

Figure 3-2   A sprinkler control system

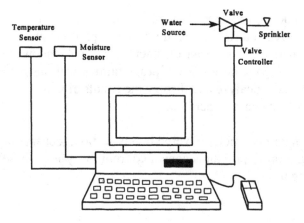

The outputs of the temperature and moisture sensors are connected to analog input channels, and the valve controller for opening and closing the valve is connected to an analog output channel. The period for when the sprinkler is turned on is set by the counter.

A fuzzy program written in NICEL for this control problem is given in Figure 3-3, and can, as described in the previous chapters, be compiled into a C program in file "sprinkle.c" containing a module named "sprinkler." This module can be called in a main program or other C modules. To use the module, the parameters need to be set for the membership functions. Figure 3-4 shows the membership functions with the specific parameters that are chosen for this example.

Figure 3-3   A fuzzy program for controlling the sprinkler

```
/* sprinkle.nl    Copyright (C) 1995 by Nicesoft Corporation */
/*
t=outdoor temperature
m=soil moisture
p=watering period
*/

membership package1(x;a,b,c,d,e,f,g)
{
  define low by triangle(0,0,a);
  define medium by triangle(b,c,d);
  define high by trapezoid(e,f,g,g);
}

membership package2(x;a,b,c,d,e,f,g,h)
{
  define short by trapezoid(0,0,a,b);
  define medium by triangle(c,d,e);
  define long by trapezoid(f,g,h,h);
}
```

procedure sprinkler(t,m;
                    p;
                    a1,b1,c1,d1,e1,f1,g1,
                    a2,b2,c2,d2,e2,f2,g2,
                    a3,b3,c3,d3,e3,f3,g3,h3)
{
 use package1(t;a1,b1,c1,d1,e1,f1,g1);
 use package1(m;a2,b2,c2,d2,e2,f2,g2);
 use package2(p;a3,b3,c3,d3,e3,f3,g3,h3);

 if m is low then p is long;
 if t is high and m is medium then p is long;
 if t is high and m is low then p is medium;
 if t is low then p is short;
}

Figure 3-4   Some specific membership functions

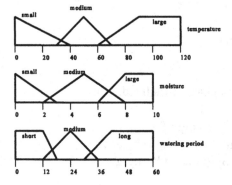

Now, a main program is written to read the temperature and
moisture inputs, call the module "sprinkler" to compute the watering
period, output an analog voltage to the valve controller to open the
valve in order to turn on the sprinkler, and start the counter. The
counter will count for the total time equal to the watering period,

and at the end of the counting, the output voltage will be set to zero to close the valve.

In LabWindows, the function to read an Analog Input and convert it into a binary code is "AI_Read." The function "AI_VScale" is then used to convert the binary code to the actual input voltage. To send electric voltage to the valve controller, the function AO_VWrite is used. To start, read and stop a counter, the functions CTR_EvCount, CTR_EvRead and CTR_Stop are used respectively. Detailed descriptions of these functions are given below:

```
AI_Read(deviceNumber,chan,gain,reading)
        input:   deviceNumber      /* assigned by config. utility */
                 chan              /* analog input channel num. */
                 gain              /* gain setting for the channel */
        output:  reading           /* result of A/D conversion */


AI_VScale(deviceNumber,chan,gain,gainAdjust,offset,reading,voltage)
        input:   deviceNumber      /* assigned by config. utility */
                 chan              /* analog input channel num. */
                 gain              /* gain setting for the channel */
                 gainAdjust        /* multiplying factor for gain */
                 offset            /* offset in reading */
                 reading           /* result of A/D conversion */
        output:  voltage           /* computed voltage */

AO_VWrite(deviceNumber,chan,voltage)
        inpu:    deviceNumber      /* assigned by config. utility */
                 chan              /* analog output channel no. */
                 voltage           /* value to be scaled and
                                      written */

CTR_EvCount(deviceNumber,ctr,timebase,cont)
        input:   deviceNumber      /* assined by config. utility */
                 ctr               /* counter number */
                 timebase          /* timebase value */
                 cont              /* if cont=1, counting continues
                                      when the counter reaches
                                      65,535, rolls over to 0,
                                      and set overflow to 0;
                                      if cont=0, counting stops
                                      when the conter reaches
                                      65,535, rolls over to 0,
                                      and set overflow to 1. */
```

```
CTR_EvRead(deviceNumber,ctr,overflow,count)
          input:   deviceNumber        /* assigned by config. utility */
                   ctr                 /* counter number */
          output:  overflow            /* overflow state of counter */
                   count               /* current total of the counter */

CTR_Stop(deviceNumber,ctr)
          input    deviceNumber        /* assigned by config. utility */
                   ctr                 /* counter number */
```

The main program is given below:

Figure 3-5   Program for controlling the sprinkler

```
#include "sprinkle.c"

main()
{
    int    brd,        /* Which board to read analog value from */
           inchan1,    /* Analog input channel for temperature */
           inchan2,    /* Analog input channel for moisture */
           outchan,    /* Analog output channel */
           gain,       /* Software-programmable gain */
           reading1,   /* Binary result of A/D conversion for temp. */
           reading2,   /* Binary result of A/D conversion for mois. */
           ctr,        /* counter number */
           timebase,
           cont,       /* continue counting? */
           overflow,          /* overflow state of the counter */
           count,             /* current total of the counter */
           total,n,m,i;
    float  temp;       /* Temperature value after scaling */
    float  mois;       /* Moisture value after scaling */
    float  period;     /* watering period */
    float  gainAdjust;       /* multiplying factor to adjust gain */
    float  offset;           /* binary offset in reading */
    float  para_1[7];        /* parameters for the membership
                                functions for temperature */
    float  para_2[7];        /* parameters for the membership
```

```
                              functions for moisture */
float  para_3[8];          /* parameters for the membership
                              functions for watering period */


brd = 1;           /* Read from board 1 */
inchan1 = 3;       /* analog input channel 3 */
inchan2 = 4;       /* analog input cahnnel 4 */
outchan = 1;       /* analog output channel 1 */
gain = 100;        /* with gain of 100 */
gainAdjust = 1;
offset = 0;
ctr = 1;           /* counter 1 */
timebase =  5;     /* 10 ms resolution */
cont = 0;          /* counting stops when the counter reaches
                        65,535, and then sets overflow to 1 */


AI_Read(brd,inchan1,gain,&reading1);
AI_VScale(brd,inchan1,gain,gainAdjust,offset,reading1,temp);

AI_Read(brd,inchan2,gain,&reading2);
AI_VScale(brd,inchan2,gain,gainAdjust,offset,reading2,mois);


/* assign parameters for the membership functions */


para_1[0] = 40;    /* a1 */
para_1[1] = 30;    /* b1 */
para_1[2] = 50;    /* c1 */
para_1[3] = 70;    /* d1 */
para_1[4] = 60;    /* e1 */
para_1[5] = 90;    /* f1 */
para_1[6] = 120;   /* g1 */
para_2[0] = 3;     /* a2 */
para_2[1] = 2;     /* b2 */
para_2[2] = 5;     /* c2 */
para_2[3] = 8;     /* d2 */
para_2[4] = 6;     /* e2 */
para_2[5] = 8;     /* f2 */
para_2[6] = 10;    /* g2 */
```

```
para_3[0] = 12;   /* a3 */
para_3[1] = 18;   /* b3 */
para_3[2] = 12;   /* c3 */
para_3[3] = 24;   /* d3 */
para_3[4] = 36;   /* e3 */
para_3[5] = 30;   /* f3 */
para_3[6] = 42;   /* g3 */
para_3[7] = 60;   /* h3 */


sprinkler("singleton",&temp,&mois,&period,para_1,para_2,
                                            para_3);
         /* use fuzzy logic to compute watering period */


AO_VWrite(brd,outchan,10);        /* output 10 V to the valve
                                     controller to open the
                                     valve */


total = 6000*period;       /* assume that period is
                              in minutes, and the counter
                              counts every 10 ms */
n = total / 65535;         /* quotient */
m = total % 65535;         /* remainder */

/* counting the total time equal to period */

for (i=1; i<=n; i++) {
      CTR_EvCount(brd,ctr,timebase,cont);
                              /* start the counter */
      overflow = 0;
      while (overflow == 0)
              CTR_EvRead(brd,ctr,overflow,count);
}
count = 0;
overflow = 0;
CTR_EvCount(brd,ctr,timebase,cont);
while (count <= m && overflow == 0)
      CTR_EvRead(brd,ctr,overflow,count);
STR_Stop(brd,ctr);
```

```
AO_VWrite(brd,outchan,0);   /* output 0 V to the valve
                               controller to close the
                               valve */
}
```

The above main program integrates the transducers, signal conditioning, and data acquisition board into a complete system. This shows that software is the most important component for coordinating all the functions. When selecting transducers, signal conditioning hardware, and data acquisition boards, be sure they meet your needs. For some specific hardware, you may need to set some variables and parameters to different values in the main program in order to achieve your specific goal.

References

National Instruments [1996] "INSTRUPEDIA 96", 6504 Bridge Point Parkway, Austin, TX 78730-5039 USA, Tel. 512-794-0100, 800-433-3488, Fax 512-794-8411.

Chapter 4   Control Systems

Today, the majority of fuzzy logic applications are in control. If you drive a new Saturn automobile with an automatic transmission, you are using fuzzy logic [Legg 1993]. Many Japanese cars use fuzzy logic in their anti-lock braking systems, cruise control, engine and emission systems, and active suspension systems. In Appendix F, some specific fuzzy logic applications in control are listed.

In a conventional approach to a control system, there is always a need to establish a correct behavioral mathematical model of the system. When the system is very complex and nonlinear, mathematical modeling can break down altogether. Even when complex mathematical equations (e.g., differential equations) are available for modeling motion, energy, pressure, flow, and temperature in a system, the computation is so complicated that a powerful computer is required. In contrast to the conventional approach, fuzzy logic is intuitive and straightforward, and its computation is simple. Therefore, fuzzy logic can be implemented on microcontrollers utilizing 8-, 16- and 32-bit processors after successfully developing a prototype on a PC platform.

There are three types of control. The purpose of Type 1 control is to achieve a vector of setpoints for a vector of output variables in minimum time without overshooting. Examples of the Type 1 control problems include battery charging, inverted pendulum, and camera focusing. In these examples, transducers/sensors measure the current values of the output variables so that they can be compared with the setpoints. The traditional Proportional Integral Differential (PID) control always uses the differences between the setpoints and the current values of the output variables to adjust control variables. A fuzzy logic controller can use the differences as well as other input variables to adjust the control variables.

Type 2 control is used to optimize a quantitative or qualitative objective function. Examples of the Type 2 control problems include welding, baking, composite curing in autoclave, and cooking. In these examples, the value of the objective function may not be easily measured. For example, in the welding application, the welding current and voltage should be controlled in order to produce the least amount of spatter. Since the spatter can not be easily measured, it is not possible to give a setpoint for it. In addition, the mathematical relationship between the spatter and welding current and voltage is complex, non-linear, and most often unknown. Therefore, PID control cannot be used in this case. However, a fuzzy logic controller from Panasonic Factory Automation [Manji 1995] is based on the observation that the shape of waves generated during routine short circuits obtained during welding has an impact on the amount of spatter. By adjusting the welding current and voltage to produce a specific wave form, the fuzzy logic controller can give a three-fold reduction in spatter.

Type 3 control is used to maneuver an object or a system to achieve a goal. Examples of the Type 3 control problems include truck docking, parallel parking, and maneuvering a fighter airplane to avoid a missile. Starting with the initial state of a system, the problem is how to apply a sequence of controls to change the state of the system in order to reach the goal.

The Inverted Pendulum Problem

Figure 4-1 depicts a classic control problem in which a pole is attached to a vehicle by a hinge such that from an upright position it can fall only to the right or left. The goal is to monitor the pole's angular position and speed and to move the vehicle left or right accordingly, so as to keep the pole upright. This means that the setpoint for the pole's angle is 0. Note that for the inverted pendulum, the shorter and/or lighter the pole, the harder the balancing act.

Figure 4-1   The Inverted Pendulum

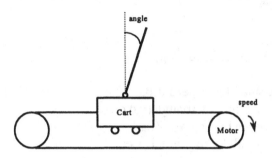

Usually, a controller for the inverted pendulum can be implemented in a microcontroller. However, in a laboratory classroom setting, it can be conveniently implemented on a PC platform. This means that a sensor that measures the pole's angle is connected to a PC, and a voltage is supplied from the PC to the motor to control the speed of the motor.

The control algorithm is based upon common sense knowledge. If the pole's angle is positive, the motor is turned positively (clockwise). If the pole's angle is negative, the motor is turned negatively (counterclockwise). The amplitude of the motor speed that is turned depends on the amplitude of the pole's angle. This common sense knowledge is easily represented by fuzzy rules shown in Figure 4-2. The fuzzy program can be compiled into a C module. Then, a main program can be written to read in the pole's angle, call the module to compute the speed of the motor, and send out a voltage to the motor to control its speed.

Figure 4-2   A fuzzy program for the inverted pendulum

/* pendulum.nl */
/* Copyright © 1996 by Nicesoft Corporation */

```
/*
ang=the pole's angle
sp=the motor speed
*/


membership pack_1(x;a,b,c,d,e,f,g,h)
{
 define positive small by trapezoid(0,0,a,b);
 define positive medium by triangle(c,d,e);
 define positive large by trapezoid(f,g,h,h);
 define negative small by trapezoid(-b,-a,0,0);
                         /* mirror image of positive small */
 define negative medium by triangle(-c,-d,-c);
                         /* mirror image of positive medium */
 define negative large by trapezoid(-h,-h,-g,-f):
                         /* mirror image of positive large */
}

procedure pedulum(ang;sp;
                    a1,b1,c1,d1,e1,f1,g1,h1,
                    a2,b2,c2,d2,e2,f2,g2,h2)
{
 use pack_1(ang;a1,b1,c1,d1,e1,f1,g1,h1);
 use pack_1(sp;a2,b2,c2,d2,e2,f2,g2,h2);

 if ang is positive/small then sp is positive/small;
 if ang is positive/medium then sp is positive/medium;
 if ang is positive/large then sp is positive/large;
 if ang is negative/small then sp is negative/small;
 if ang is negative/medium then sp is negative/medium;
 if ang is negative/large then sp is negative/medium;
}
```

The above inverted pendulum has one pole. To make the problem
more difficult, consider controlling a two-pole inverted pendulum as
shown in Figure 4-3. The strategy for controlling the two-pole

inverted pendulum is to first move the cart to align the two poles into a straight line, and then move the cart according to the one-pole strategy as described above.

Figure 4-3   The Two-Pole Inverted Pendulum

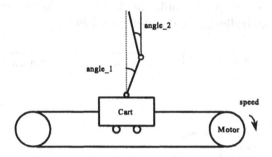

The Hitachi Ping-Pong Ball Controller

In [Hitachi 1993], a demonstration project as shown in Figure 4-4 shows how a ping-pong ball is pushed up through a tube by a fan at the bottom. The input variables to the fuzzy logic ping-pong ball controller are Error and Direction, where Error is the difference between the ball's position and the selected setpoint, and Direction is the difference in Error between the current sample and the last one. The output variable is the fan's Speed. The mathematical relationship between Speed and Error and Direction is complex and non-linear due to the following factors:

(1) The time delay that occurs between a speed change command and the resulting change in air flow is about 1 to 2 seconds.

(2) The fan can easily overpower the ball's inertia.
(3) The system responds asymmetrically to move-up and move-down commands.

However, if fuzzy logic is used, the complex mathematical relationship is not needed. Based upon common sense knowledge, one can achieve a very good result. The detail of the fuzzy logic ping-pong ball controller is given in [Hitachi 1993].

Figure 4-4   The Hitachi Ping-Pong Ball Control Demonstration

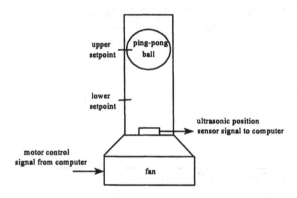

A Comparison of Fuzzy Logic vs PID Control

The traditional Proportional Integral Differential (PID) control can only be applied to the Type 1 control problems with a single output variable. The goal is to reach a setpoint for the output variable. Let E be the difference between the current value at time n and the setpoint of the output variable. The PID control adjusts an input (control) variable X at time n+1 according to the following formula:

$$X = K1*E + K2*\Sigma E + K3*\Delta E$$

where K1, K2, and K3 are constants, ΣE is the sum of E at time 0
through time n, and ΔE is the difference between E at time n and E
at time n-1. The PID control works well only when the relationship
between the input variables and output variable is linear. If it is non-
linear, K1, K2, and K3 will not be constant. Even when the
relationship is linear, a correct mathematical linear model is still
needed to compute the correct K1, K2, and K3.

The first, second, and third term in the above formula are called a
Proportional term, an Integral term, and a Differential term,
respectively. Increasing K1 improves the dynamic and static
accuracy of the system, but if K1 is too large, it can cause
oscillation. An increase in K2 increases the static stability of the
system, but if K2 is too large, it can cause overshoot and oscillation
around the setpoint. The differential term prevents the proportional
and integral terms from overdriving the system and causing
oscillations.

Figure 4-5   Performance of controllers

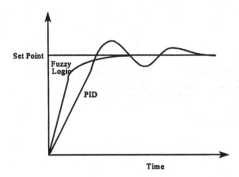

Fuzzy logic methodology does not need a complex mathematical model. It is intuitive, and completely based upon common sense knowledge. To the uninitiated, fuzzy logic may look simple. However, don't be confused with the word "fuzzy." The fuzzy logic method is mathematically precise, and can be used to handle nonlinearities and produce good results. In many practical applications, fuzzy logic controllers perform better than PID controllers. A fuzzy logic controller can reach a setpoint sooner than a PID controller with minimum overshoot as shown in Figure 4-5.

Process Control and Product Quality Control

What is a process? Simply put it, a process is an operation of a setup that is intended to manufacture a product. For example, consider the rolling mill shown in Figure 4-6. It produces a continuous sheet of some material at a certain rate.

Figure 4-6   A simplified rolling mill

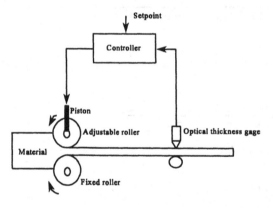

A feedback controller moves a piston to modify the gap between a pair of rollers that squeezes the material into the desired thickness.

The thickness of the sheet, called a process variable, is an input variable to the controller. The desired thickness is a setpoint for the process variable. The controller takes the error, which is the difference between the current value and the setpoint of the process variable, and adjusts the piston accordingly.

The most difficult problem to overcome with a feedback controller is process deadtime – the delay between the application of a control effort and its first effect on the process variable [Vandoren 1996]. In Figure 4-6, the deadtime is caused by the distance between the roller and the thickness gage. This means that after the controller commands to move the piston to change the gap between the rollers, the thickness gage will only see the change after some specific time period. If the controller expects a result any sooner, it will determine that its last control effort had no effect and will continue to apply even larger corrections to the rollers until the sensor begins to see the thickness changing in the desired direction. By that time, however, it will be too late. The controller will have already overcompensated for the original thickness error, perhaps to the point of causing an even larger error in the opposite direction. This is the so-called oscillation problem. In general, it is very difficult for a PID controller to handle process deadtime effectively. A fuzzy logic controller, however, is well equipped to handle this problem. Figure 4-7 shows a fuzzy program that implements the fuzzy logic controller, where the correct set of parameters for the membership functions can be chosen to get a good control result. If it is necessary, the fuzzy program can be modified by using additional input variables such as roller speed.

Figure 4-7   A fuzzy program for the rolling mill

```
/* mill.nl */
/* Copyright © 1996 by Nicesoft Corporation */
```

```
/*
error=difference between the current value and setpoint of the sheet
        thickness;
displ=the vertical displacement of the piston from its current
        position.
*/

membership pack_1(x;a,b,c,d,e,f,g,h)
{
 define positive small by trapezoid(0,0,a,b);
 define positive medium by triangle(c,d,e);
 define positive large by trapezoid(f,g,h,h);
 define negative small by trapezoid(-b,-a,0,0);
                            /* mirror image of positive small */
 define negative medium by triangle(-e,-d,-c);
                            /* mirror image of positive medium */
 define negative large by trapezoid(-h,-h,-g,-f):
                            /* mirror image of positive large */
}

procedure mill(error;displ;
                a1,b1,c1,d1,e1,f1,g1,h1,
                a2,b2,c2,d2,e2,f2,g2,h2)
{
 use pack_1(error;a1,b1,c1,d1,e1,f1,g1,h1);
 use pack_1(displ;a2,b2,c2,d2,e2,f2,g2,h2);

 if error is positive/small then displ is negative/small;
 if error is positive/medium then displ is negative/medium;
 if error is positive/large then displ is negative/large;
 if error is negative/small then displ is positive/small;
 if error is negative/medium then displ is positive/medium;
 if error is negative/large then displ is positive/medium;
}
```

Process control, described in the above example, focuses on
producing products. Product quality control is another type of

control which focuses on product quality [Barnes 1996, Agres 1996, Studt 1994]. As shown in Figure 4-8, product quality control automatically generates setpoints for a process control. The process control performs efficiently to reach the setpoints. However, incorrect setpoints can cause a process to produce poor quality products. For example, an air condtioning system operates according to a set temperature. The conditioned air flow is the product from the air conditioning system. The quality is how a person feels from the air flow. If the temperature is set too high, the person may still feel hot. If the temperature is set too low, the person may feel too cold. Another example is baking a cake. If the temperature is set too high and the time too long, the cake will come out burnt. If the temperature is set too low and the time too short, the cake will not be done.

Figure 4-8   Hybrid-based control

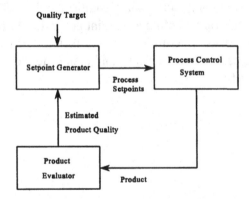

In Figure 4-8, the product evaluator may be a quality assurance (QA) engineer or a software. The QA engineer can inspect a product and give his evaluation. For example, he may eat the cake in the cake-baking example. Of course, the QA engineer can also use instruments to measure product parameters before he makes his evaluation. Usually, this kind of evaluation process is manual and is time-consuming. The manufaturing process operator may not have time to wait for the QA's results in order to adjust process setpoints. Therefore, it may be desirable to implement the product evaluator in software. It may take product parameters such as the sheet thickness in the rolling mill example and/or the process setpoints as input variables, and implement an objective function of the product. The objective function may be the overall evaluation of multiple criteria for the product itself and for the manufacturing process such as low cost, high efficiency, low pollution, etc. It may also be subjective. For example, in the cake-baking example, the quality of the cake is based on the opinion of the person who eats the cake. In any case, the objective function can be implemented by a fuzzy program where the output variable is the "goodness" of the product. As it will be discussed in Chapter 8, fuzzy rules in the fuzzy program may be obtained by first collecting data for products produced with various setpoints, and then analyzing patterns in the collected data. This data will also be useful for implementing a setpoint generator. For example, in the cake-baking example, several cakes can be baked at different temperatures and time setpoints and then tasted to determine their qualities.

The Truck Docking Problem

The truck docking problem was introduced by Nguyen and Widrow [1989], who demonstrated that a neural network could be trained to back a truck to a dock. Kong and Kosko [1992] obtained functionally equivalent results by representing the neural network behavior with fuzzy functions. Wiggins [1992] showed that the problem could be solved using the genetic algorithm coupled directly to fuzzy functions. The genetic algorithm can be used to find a minimal pathway from a starting location to the dock in the presence of constraints by searching for parameters for membership functions in a fuzzy program. In this section, a method on how to write a fuzzy program for the truck docking problem will be covered. Machine training to adjust parameters of membership functions will be discussed in Chapter 9.

As shown in Figure 4-9, the truck docking problem is described as follows: Given the location and direction of the truck, we want to know how to set the steering wheel for a short backward movement. Then, from the new location and direction of the truck, the steering wheel is set again. This incremental process is repeated until the truck arrives at the dock.

Figure 4-9   The truck docking problem

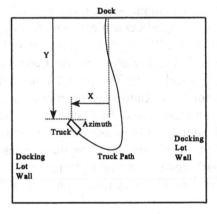

The X and Y axises are the vertical and horizontal lines passing through the middle of the dock, respectively. The location of the truck is given by (X,Y), where X and Y are the distances from the Y and X axises to the truck, respectively. The direction of the truck is measured by the azimuth value. The X values are assumed to range from -50 on the left to 50 on the right. The values of the steering wheel angle are assumed to range from 30 on the far left to -30 on the far right. It is also assumed that the truck is in a starting position that will allow it to move backward without hitting the wall, and that it has some distance away from the dock so that the steering instructions do not depend on the Y value of the truck.

The truck docking problem is different from the Type 1 control problem. Unlike the Type 1 control problem where the target (setpoint) can always be set, only the local information, the X and azimuth of the truck, can be used to steer the wheel of the truck. The way to approach this problem is to imagine that there is a function mapping from the X and azimuth to the steering wheel angle, and to assume that there is a look-up table representing this function. Then, the controller can take cues from the look-up table which dictates what steering wheel angle to set for every combination of the X and azimuth values. In reality, this function is not known. Even when it is known, the complete look-up table will be so large that it makes it inefficient to use.

The fuzzy logic approach is to introduce fuzzy quantifications for the X, azimuth, and steering wheel angle, and then to approximate the function by fuzzy rules. We begin with a partial look-up table showing some values of X and azimuth and their corresponding values of the steeting wheel angle. This partial look-up table can be obtained from common sense knowledge or from actual data collected by having an experienced driver performing a few runs of truck-dockings and automatically measuring the X, azimuth and steering wheel angle through sensors during the courses of the truck-dockings. Figure 4-10 shows such a table. Note that a detailed discussion on how to discover fuzzy rules from data will be given in Chapter 8.

Figure 4-10   A partial look-up table

X	Azimuth	Steering Wheel Angle
-30	-90	-30
-10	-90	-30
10	-90	30
30	-90	30
-30	-45	-30
-10	-45	-30
10	-45	-30
30	-45	30
-30	0	0
-10	0	-5
10	0	-30
30	0	-30
-30	45	0
-10	45	0
10	45	-20
30	45	-30
-30	90	30
-10	90	15
10	90	-15
30	90	-30

In the above table, only rows whose azimuth values range from -90 to 90 are listed. Steering wheel angles for the truck azimuth that do not fall within this range can be computed from the table. For example, if the truck azimuth is 135, its steering wheel angle for a given X is the mirror image of the steering wheel angle for the case whose azimuth is 45 with respect to X. Similarly, the case for 180 is the mirror image of the case for 0.

The next step is to fuzzify the table shown in Figure 4-10. For example, since the domain of X is [-30,30], if X is 30, it is fuzzified to "positive large." The fuzzified table is shown in Figure 4-11, in which each unique row represents a fuzzy rule. Note that a method for minimizing the number of fuzzy rules will be discussed in Chapter 8.

Figure 4-11   The fuzzified table of Figure 4-10

X	Azimuth	Steering Wheel Angle
negative large	negative large	negative large
negative small	negative large	negative large
positive small	negative large	positive large
positive large	negative large	positive large
negative large	negative medium	negative large
negative small	negative medium	negative large
positive small	negative medium	negative large
positive large	negative medium	positive large
negative large	zero	zero
negative small	zero	negative small
positive small	zero	negative large

positive large	zero	negative large
negative large	positive medium	zero
negative small	positive medium	zero
positive small	positive medium	negative medium
positive large	positive medium	negative large
negative large	positive large	positive large
negative small	positive large	positive medium
positive small	positive large	negative medium
positive large	positive large	negative large

In Figure 4-11, the fuzzy quatifications "negative large," "negative medium," "negative small," "zero," "positive small," "positive medium," and "positive large" have to be defined. A complete fuzzy program is shown in Figure 4-12.

Figure 4-12   A fuzzy program for the truck docking problem

```
/* docking.nl */
/*
Copyright © 1996 by Nicesoft Corporation
*/

/*
x=the X coordinate of the truck;
az=the truck azimuth;
steer=the truck steering wheel angle.
*/

membership pack_1(var;a,b,c,d,e,f,g,h)
{
  define zero by triangle(-a,0,a);
  define positive small by triangle(0,0,b);
  define positive medium by triangle(c,d,e);
  define positive large by trapezoid(f,g,h,h);
```

```
define negative small by triangle(-b,0,0);
                                /* mirror image of positive small */
define negative medium by triangle(-e,-d,-c);
                                /* mirror image of positive medium */
define negative large by trapezoid(-h,-h,-g,-f):
                                /* mirror image of positive large */
}

procedure docking(x,az;steer;
                a1,b1,c1,d1,e1,f1,g1,h1,
                a2,b2,c2,d2,e2,f2,g2,h2,
                a3,b3,c3,d3,e3,f3,g3,h3)
{
 use pack_1(x;a1,b1,c1,d1,e1,f1,g1,h1);
 use pack_1(az;a2,b2,c2,d2,e2,f2,g2,h2);
 use pack_1(steer;a3,b3,c3,d3,e3,f3,g3,h3);

 if x is negative/large and az is negative/large then steer is negative/large;
 if x is negative/small and az is negative/large then steer is negative/large;
 if x is positive/small and az is negative/large then steer is positive/large;
 if x is positive/large and az is negative/large then steer is positive/large;

 if x is negative/large and az is negative/medium then steer is negative/large;
 if x is negative/small and az is negative/medium then steer is negative/large;
 if x is positive/small and az is negative/medium then steer is negative/large;
 if x is positive/large and az is negative/medium then steer is positive/large;

 if x is negative/large and az is zero then steer is zero;
 if x is negative/small and az is zero then steer is negative/small;
 if x is positive/small and az is zero then steer is negative/large;
 if x is positive/large and az is zero then steer is negative/large;

 if x is negative/large and az is positive/medium then steer is zero;
 if x is negative/small and az is positive/medium then steer is zero;
 if x is positive/small and az is positive/medium then steer is negative/medium;
 if x is positive/large and az is positive/medium then steer is negative/large;

 if x is negative/large and az is positive/large then steer is positive/large;
 if x is negative/small and az is positive/large then steer is positive/medium;
 if x is positive/small and az is positive/large then steer is negative/medium;
 if x is positive/large and az is positive/large then steer is negative/large;
}
```

The Evasive Maneuvers Problem

The evasive maneuvers problem was given in [Erickson and Zytkow 1988, Schultz and Grefenstette 1990]. There are two objects in this problem, a plane and a missile. The objective is to maneuver the plane to avoid being hit by the approaching missile. The missile tracks the motion of the plane and steers toward the plane's anticipated position. The initial speed of the missile is greater than that of the plane, but the missile loses speed as it maneuvers. If the missile speed drops below some threshold, it loses maneuverability and drops out of the sky. There are six sensors measuring the following variables:

VARIABLE	DESCRIPTION
turn	The current turning rate of the plane.
time	Time since the detection of the missile.
range	The missile's current distance from the plane.
bearing	The direction from the plane to the missile.
heading	The missile's direction relative to the plane.
speed	The missile's current speed.

The current values of these variables represent a state. The control decision is performed incrementally. This means that given a state, the controller will take "time," "range," "bearing," "heading," and "speed" as the input variables, and compute the value for the output variable "turn" which tells the plane how much to turn and what direction to turn to. As a result of the plane's action, a new state is entered, and a new control cycle is started again. This control process is repeated until either the plane is hit or the missile is exhausted.

We assume that the domain of the variable "turn" is [-180,180] where -V and V in the interval means to turn V degrees right and left, respectively. The other variables are defined as shown in Figure 4-13, where the small square and circle represent the plane and the missile respectively, and the arrows indicate their directions. The plane's direction is the X axis. The domain for both "bearing" and "heading" is [-180,180]. We assume that the domain of the variable "range" is [0,2000], and that the domain of the variable "speed" is [0,1000].

Figure 4-13   Definitions of the variables "bearing" and "heading"

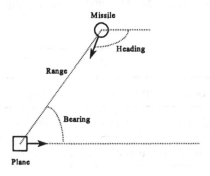

In [Schultz and Grefenstette 1990], seven rules using interval conditions are given to control the plane in a simulation. These rules are based upon the following observations:

    (1)   If the missile is far enough away, turn so that it is behind the plane.

    (2)   When the missile is closing in, make hard turns such that the missile loses velocity.

    (3)   If the missile is heading away from the plane and moving slowly, ignore it and continue in the current direction.

It is more intuitive and straightforward to implement the above strategy by fuzzy rules. Figure 4-14 is a fuzzy program which is intended to duplicate the results of Schultz and Grefenstette. Note that in the "use" statements of the fuzzy program, the same parameters are used for "bearing," "heading," and "turn" since they have the same domain. Also, without loss of completeness, the fuzzy rules are given only for the cases where values of the variable "bearing" are in [0,180], since the cases where values of "bearing" are in [-180,0] are the mirror image of the ones in [0,180]. For example, if "bearing" is -B and "heading" is H, first use B and -H to call the fuzzy procedure to compute the value T of the variable "turn," and then use -T to control the plane's turn.

Figure 4-14   A fuzzy program for the evasive maneuvers problem

```
/* plane.nl */
/*
Copyright © 1996 by Nicesoft Corporation
*/

/*
turn=turn;
rg=range;
br=bearing;
hd=heading;
sp=speed.
*/

membership pack_1(x;a,b,c,d,e,f,g,h)
{
  define positive small by trapezoid(0,0,a,b);
  define positive medium by triangle(c,d,e);
  define positive large by trapezoid(f,g,h,h);
  define negative small by trapezoid(-b,-a,0,0);
                          /* mirror image of positive small */
  define negative medium by triangle(-e,-d,-c);
                          /* mirror image of positive medium */
  define negative large by trapezoid(-h,-h,-g,-f):
                          /* mirror image of positive large */
}
```

```
membership pack_2(x;a,b,c,d,e,f,g,h)
{
 define small by trapezoid(0,0,a,b);
 define medium by triangle(c,d,e);
 define large by trapezoid(f,g,h,h);
}

procedure plane(rg,br,hd,sp;turn;
                a1,b1,c1,d1,e1,f1,g1,h1,
                a2,b2,c2,d2,e2,f2,g2,h2,
                a3,b3,c3,d3,e3,f3,g3,h3)
{
 use pack_2(rg;a1,b1,c1,d1,e1,f1,g1,h1);
 use pack_1(br;a2,b2,c2,d2,e2,f2,g2,h2);
 use pack_1(hd;a2,b2,c2,d2,e2,f2,g2,h2);
 use pack_2(sp;a3,b3,c3,d3,e3,f3,g3,h3);
 use pack_1(turn;a2,b2,c2,d2,e2,f2,g2,h2);

 if rg is small and br is positive/large and
    hd is negative/small then turn is negative/medium;
              /* if missile is close behind and slightly to left,
                 make about 90 degree turn to right. */


 if rg is large and br is positive/large and
    hd is negative/small then turn is negative/small;
              /* if missile is far behind and slightly to left,
                 let it get closer. */

 if rg is large and br is positive/medium and
    hd is negative/medium then turn is negative/medium;
              /* if missile is coming from left,
                 make about 90 degree turn right. */
```

if br is positive/small and
    hd is negative/large then turn is negative/large;
        /* if missile is coming from front,
           make about 180 degree turn right. */

if br is positive/large and hd is positive/large and
    sp is small then turn is negative/small;
        /* if missile is heading away and going slow,
          just go straight. */
}

_____

References

Barnes, R. [1996] "Hybrid-based PLC control predicts, optimizes product quality," *Control Engineering*, June 1996, pp.75-78.

Electronic Design [1994] "Neural network/fuzzy-logic technology enables intelligent and fast battery-charger circuit," *Electronic Design*, May 1, 1995, pp.38-40.

Erickson, M.D., and Zytkow, J.M. [1988] "Utilizing experience for improving the tactical manager," *Proceedings of the Fifth International Conference on Machine Learning*, Ann Arbor, MI, pp. 444-450.

Hitachi [1993] "Fuzzy logic application note," Order number M20P002A, Hitachi America, Ltd., Semiconductor & I.C. Division, San Francisco Center, 2000 Sierra Point Parkway, Brisbane, CA 94005-1819, USA, Tel. (415) 589-8300. *This note describes a demonstration project for moving a ping-pong ball up and down vertically inside a tube to one of two setpoints by the rising column of air generated by a fan at the bottom of the tube.*

Jurgen, R. [1995] "The Electronic motorist," *IEEE Spectrum*, March 1995, pp. 37048.

Kong, S.G., and Kosko, B. [1992] "Comparison of fuzzy and neural truck backer-upper control systems," in *Neural Networks and Fuzzy Systems*, New York: Prentice Hall, 1992.

Legg, G. [1993] "Transmission's fuzzy logic keeps you on track," *EDN*, December 23, 1993, pp. 60-63.

Manji, J.F. [1995] "Fuzzy logic creates new applications," *Managing Automation*, August 1995, pp. 49-51.

May, G.S. [1994] "Manufacturing ICs the neural way," *IEEE Spectrum*, September 1994, pp. 47-51.

Nguyen, D., and Widrow, B. [1989] "The truck backer-upper: An example of self-learning in neural networks," *Proceedings of International Conference on Neural Networks*, June 1989, pp. 357-363.

Rocha, A.F., Morooka, C.K., and Alegre, L. [1996] "Smart oil recovery," *IEEE Spectrum*, July 1996, pp. 48-51.

Schultz, A.C., and Grefenstette, J.J. [1990] "Improving tactical plans with genetic algorithm," *Proceedings of the 2nd International IEEE Conference on Tools for Artificial Intelligence*, IEEE Catalog Number 90CH2915-7, IEEE Computer Society, Customer Service Center, 10662 Los Vaqueros Circle, P.O. Box 3014, Los Alamitos, CA 90720-1264, USA, pp. 328-334.

Studt, T. [1994] "Artificial intelligence software optimizes process models," *R & D Magazine*, July 1994, pp. 37.

Tremaine, B.P. [1994] "Weigh the benefits of fuzzy-logic vs classical control in a disk-drive spindle," _EDN_, July 7, 1994, pp. 137-144.

Vandoren, V.J. [1996] "The Smith Predictor: A process engineer's crystal ball," _Control Engineering_, May 1996, pp. 61-82.

Vieira, P., and Gomide, F. [1996] "Computer-aided train dispatch," _IEEE Spectrum_, July 1996, pp.51-53.

Washington Technology [1994] "A warm fuzzy for environmental monitoring," _Washinton Technology_, March 24, 1994.

Wiggins, R. [1992] "Docking a truck: A genetic fuzzy approach," _AI Expert_, May 1992, pp. 28-35.

Williams, T. [1991] "Fuzzy logic simplifies complex control problems," _Computer Design_, March 1, 1991, pp. 90-99.

Chapter 5   Pattern Recognition

Pattern recognition is a field of classifying objects into classes or categories. For example, voice recognition classifies voices into words, and handwriting recognition classifies handwritings into letters, digits, or words. Each object (pattern) is usually represented by a set of feature (attribute) values.

Many problems can be treated as pattern recognition problems. For example, consider resource allocation in project management and business reengineering. A list of resources needs to be allocated to a list of activitities. In this case, the resources can be treated as patterns and the activities can be treated as classes.

NICEL in *Decision Plus* [Nicesoft Corporation 1994] is a very convenient language that can be used to represent a solution for a pattern recognition problem. Let attributes of a pattern be input variables, and classes c1,...,cn be output variables. The domain of these output variables is [0,1]. Figure 5-1 is a simple fuzzy program that classifies an employee into one of the two classes, Class1 or Class2, according to his years of education, years of experience, and hourly wage.

Figure 5-1   A Fuzzy Program for Pattern Recognition

```
/* classify.nl */
/*
Copyright © 1996 by Nicesoft Corporation
*/

/*
edu=Employee's year of education;
exp=Employee's year of experience;
w=Employee's hourly wage;
class1=Class 1;
class2=Class 2;
*/
```

```
membership pack_1(x;a,b,c,d,e,f,g,h)
{
    define low by trapezoid(0,0,a,b);
    define medium by triangle(c,d,e);
    define high by trapezoid(f,g,h,h);
}

procedure classify(edu,exp,w;
                class1,class2;
                a1,b1,c1,d1,e1,f1,g1,h1,
                a2,b2,c2,d2,e2,f2,g2,h2,
                a3,b3,c3,d3,e3,f3,g3,h3)

{
    use pack_1(edu;a1,b1,c1,d1,e1,f1,g1,h1);
    use pack_1(exp;a1,b1,c1,d1,e1,f1,g1,h1);
    use pack_1(w;a2,b2,c2,d2,e2,f2,g2,h2);
    use pack_1(class1;a3,b3,c3,d3,e3,f3,g3,h3);
    use pack_1(class2;a3,b3,c3,d3,e3,f3,g3,h3);

    if edu is high and exp is high then class1 is high;
    if edu is medium and exp is high and w is medium
        then class1 is medium;
    if edu is low then class1 is low;
    if exp is low then class1 is low;

    if w is low then class2 is high;
    if exp is low then class2 is high;
    if edu is high and w is high then class2 is low;
}
```

This fuzzy program is first compiled into a module in a target language. Then, a main program is written to read in an employee's years of education, years of experience, and hourly wage as the input values, and call the procedure "classify" to compute the values of the output variables, class1 and class2, and assign him to the class whose output value is the largest and/or greater than a specified threshold. For example, if class1 > class2 and class1 > Δ where Δ is a non-negative threshold, then the employee is classified into Class1. If class2 > class1 and class2 > Δ, then the employee is classified into Class2. Otherwise, the classification is unknown.

In Figure 5-1, if it is known that the membership functions for "low" and "high" do not overlap, then those rules that define either "class1 is low" or "class2 is low" can be dropped. Therefore, Figure 5-1 can be simplified to Figure 5-2.

Figure 5-2   A Simplified Fuzzy Program of Figure 5-1

```
/* classify.nl */
/*
Copyright © 1996 by Nicesoft Corporation
*/


/*
edu=Employee's year of education;
exp=Employee's year of experience;
w=Employee's hourly wage;
class1=Class 1;
class2=Class 2;
*/
membership pack_1(x;a,b,c,d,e,f,g,h)
{
    define low by trapezoid(0,0,a,b);
    define medium by triangle(c,d,e);
    define high by trapezoid(f,g,h,h);
}

procedure classify(edu,exp,w;
                class1,class2;
                a1,b1,c1,d1,e1,f1,g1,h1,
                a2,b2,c2,d2,e2,f2,g2,h2,
                a3,b3,c3,d3,e3,f3,g3,h3)
{
    use pack_1(edu;a1,b1,c1,d1,e1,f1,g1,h1);
```

```
    use pack_1(exp;a1,b1,c1,d1,e1,f1,g1,h1);
    use pack_1(w;a2,b2,c2,d2,e2,f2,g2,h2);
    use pack_1(class1;a3,b3,c3,d3,e3,f3,g3,h3);
    use pack_1(class2;a3,b3,c3,d3,e3,f3,g3,h3);

    if edu is high and exp is high then class1 is high;
    if edu is medium and exp is high and w is medium
        then class1 is medium;

    if w is low then class2 is high;
    if exp is low then class2 is high;
}
```

The above fuzzy programs basically use fuzzy rules to define membership functions of Class1 and Class2. A pattern is assigned to the class whose membership function has the highest value. If there is just a 2-class pattern recognition problem such as classifying an employee as a skilled or not skilled worker, there is no need to specify fuzzy rules for Class2. Figure 5-3 shows such a fuzzy program. In this case, a pattern is assigned to Class1 if class1 $> \Delta$. Otherwise, it is assigned to Class2.

Figure 5-3   A Further Simplified Fuzzy Program of Figure 5-2

```
/* classify.nl */
/*
Copyright © 1996 by Nicesoft Corporation
*/

/*
edu=Employee's year of education;
exp=Employee's year of experience;
w=Employee's hourly wage;
class1=Class 1;
*/
```

```
membership pack_1(x;a,b,c,d,e,f,g,h)
{
    define low by trapezoid(0,0,a,b);
    define medium by triangle(c,d,e);
    define high by trapezoid(f,g,h,h);
}

procedure classify(edu,exp,w;
                class1;
                a1,b1,c1,d1,e1,f1,g1,h1,
                a2,b2,c2,d2,e2,f2,g2,h2,
                a3,b3,c3,d3,e3,f3,g3,h3)

{
    use pack_1(edu;a1,b1,c1,d1,e1,f1,g1,h1);
    use pack_1(exp;a1,b1,c1,d1,e1,f1,g1,h1);
    use pack_1(w;a2,b2,c2,d2,e2,f2,g2,h2);
    use pack_1(class1;a3,b3,c3,d3,e3,f3,g3,h3);

    if edu is high and exp is high then class1 is high;
    if edu is medium and exp is high and w is medium
        then class1 is medium;
}
```

Fuzzy logic has been applied to many pattern recognition problems. In this book, some specific fuzzy logic applications in pattern recognition are listed in Appendix G.

Determination of Air Pollution Categories

The existing guideline for public reporting of daily air quality is based upon a Pollutant Standards Index (PSI) [Hunt et al. 1976, Ott 1978]. Depending upon various PSI ranges, five pollution categories such as Good, Moderate, Unhealthful, Very Unhealthful, and Hazardous can be defined. Figure 5-4 is an example of these categories [Chen and Chang 1995].

Figure 5-4   Numerical PSI ranges for air pollution categories

PSI Range	Air Pollution Category
0 - 50	Good
51 - 100	Moderate
101 - 199	Unhealthful
200 - 209	Very Unhealthful
300 - 500	Hazardous

Figure 5-5   A table for computing PSI

PSI	SO_2 average over 24 hours	CO average over 8 hours	O_3 average over 1 hour	NO_2 average over 1 hour	PM_{10} average over 24 hours
0	0.00	0.0	0.00	0.00	0
50	0.03	4.5	0.05	0.15	50
100	0.14	9.0	0.12	0.30	150
200	0.30	15	0.20	0.60	350
300	0.60	30	0.40	1.20	420
400	0.80	40	0.50	1.60	500
500	1.00	50	0.60	2.00	600

Currently, PSI is computed by first measuring the SO_2, CO, O_3, NO_2 and PM_{10} contents in the air and then looking it up in the table as proposed by Taiwan EPA, as shown in Figure 5-5. A subindex is computed for each of these five measurements, and the maximum of the subindices determines the PSI. If a measured value is not in the table, a linear interpolation is used to compute a subindex.

The problem with the current PSI approach is that small changes in the measurements may report different air pollution categories. For example, if CO increases from 14.9 ppm to 15 ppm, the PSI will change from 199 to 200, and cause the air pollution category to change from "unhealthful" to "very unhealthful." To remedy this problem, a Fuzzy Pollutant Standards Index (FPSI) was proposed in [Chen and Chang 1995]. In this section, the use of an index will be avoided altogether. Pollutant measurements will be directly related to the air pollution categories by treating it as a pattern recognition problem.

The above air pollution classification problem will be treated as a five-class pattern recognition problem. A fuzzy program for this problem is given in Figure 5-6, which will be compiled into a module in a target language. Given some values of so2, co, o3, no2, and pm, we can call the procedure "pollute" to compute the values of the output variables gd, md, uh, vuh, and haz. The most severe category among those output variables whose values are greater than a threshold Δ will be the air pollution category that is reported. For example, if gd=0.8, md=0.75, uh=0.74, vuh=0.4, haz=0.0, and Δ=0.7, it will be reported that the air is "unhealthful." This class-assigning scheme is different from the one where a pattern is assigned to the class whose output value is the largest. In fact, depending upon applications, different class-assigning schemes can be used. Note that the tables shown in Figure 5-4 and Figure 5-5 can be consulted to set correct parameters for the membership functions in the fuzzy program.

Figure 5-6   A Fuzzy Program for Determining Air Pollution
              Categories

```
/* pollute.nl */
/* Copyright © 1996 by Nicesoft Corporation */

/*
so2=SO₂ measurement;
co=CO measurement;
o3=O₃ measurement;
no2=NO₂ measurement;
pm=PM₁₀ measurement;
gd=Category "Good";
md=Category "Moderate";
uh=Category "Unhealthful";
vuh=Category "Very Unhealthful";
haz=Category "Hazardous";
*/

membership pack_1(x;a,b,c,d,e,f,g,h,m)
{
    define very_low by trapezoid(0,0,a,b);
    define low by triangle(c,d,e);
    define medium by triangle(c+m,d+m,e+m);
    define high by triangle(c+2*m,d+2*m,e+2*m);
    define very_high by trapezoid(f,g,h,h);
}

membership pack_2(x;a,b,c,d,e,f,g,h)
{
    define low by trapezoid(0,0,a,b);
    define medium by triangle(c,d,e);
    define high by trapezoid(f,g,h,h);
}
```

```
procedure pollute(so2,co,o3,no2,pm;
                gd,md,uh,vuh,haz;
                a1,b1,c1,d1,e1,f1,g1,h1,m1,
                a2,b2,c2,d2,e2,f2,g2,h2,m2,
                a3,b3,c3,d3,e3,f3,g3,h3,m3,
                a4,b4,c4,d4,e4,f4,g4,h4,m4,
                a5,b5,c5,d5,e5,f5,g5,h5,m5,
                a6,b6,c6,d6,e6,f6,g6,h6)
{
    use pack_1(so2;a1,b1,c1,d1,e1,f1,g1,h1,m1);
    use pack_1(co;a2,b2,c2,d2,e2,f2,g2,h2,m2);
    use pack_1(o3;a3,b3,c3,d3,e3,f3,g3,h3,m3);
    use pack_1(no2;a4,b4,c4,d4,e4,f4,g4,h4,m4);
    use pack_1(pm;a5,b5,c5,d5,e5,f5,g5,h5,m5);
    use pack_2(gd;a6,b6,c6,d6,e6,f6,g6,h6);
    use pack_2(md;a6,b6,c6,d6,e6,f6,g6,h6);
    use pack_2(uh;a6,b6,c6,d6,e6,f6,g6,h6);
    use pack_2(vuh;a6,b6,c6,d6,e6,f6,g6,h6);
    use pack_2(haz;a6,b6,c6,d6,e6,f6,g6,h6);

    if so2 is very_low then gd is high;
    if co is very_low then gd is high;
    if  o3 is very_low then gd is high;
    if no2 is very_low then gd is high;
    if pm is very_low then gd is high;

    if so2 is low then md is high;
    if co is low then md is high;
    if  o3 is low then md is high;
    if no2 is low then md is high;
    if pm is low then md is high;

    if so2 is medium then uh is high;
    if co is medium then uh is high;
    if  o3 is medium then uh is high;
    if no2 is medium then uh is high;
    if pm is medium then uh is high;
```

```
    if so2 is high then vuh is high;
    if co is high then vuh is high;
    if  o3 is high then vuh is high;
    if no2 is high then vuh is high;
    if pm is high then vuh is high;

    if so2 is very_high then haz is high;
    if co is very_high then haz is high;
    if  o3 is very_high then haz is high;
    if no2 is very_high then haz is high;
    if pm is very_high then haz is high;
}
```

Digital Signal Processing

Since many applications in pattern recognition involve either classifying a signal or waveform into classes or detecting the presence of certain patterns in the signal, Digital Signal Processing (DSP) such as the Fast Fourier Transform (FFT) and filtering will be briefly discussed in this section.

In the 1960s, a group of engineers and mathematicians working at AT&T Bell Labs invented a set of techniques known as digital signal processing (DSP). The problem they were working on was the recovery of information from distorted, noisy, incomplete, and ambiguous signals caused by data transmission over long-distance phone lines and satellite links. The algorithms they invented are used today in many fields, including stereo-sound electronics, medical imaging, high-speed communications, and servo controllers. In this section, only DSP functions that are useful for pattern recognition of signals will be discussed.

Before classifying a waveform, it is necessary to extract features (parameters) from it. The features can be extracted in the time domain or in the frequency domain. In the former case, algorithms are written to process the sampled data of the waveform, while in the latter case, the waveform is decomposed into component waveforms by a bank of bandpass filters and then features are extracted from the component waveforms. Figure 5-7 shows some decomposition approaches commonly used. Note that Figure 5-7(b) is related to wavelet decomposition [Morgan 1996].

A general approach to process a waveform is to divide it into consecutive frames, where each frame is a segment of the waveform for a specified time duration, e.g, 10 to 20 milliseconds (ms) in speech recognition. Many methods can be used to extract features of a frame. For example, the amplitude/energy and zero crossing/frequency parameters of the frame can be computed, and then used as its features. The segmentation problem for a waveform is to use the features of frames to merge similar consecutive frames into a larger segment.

Figure 5-7   Some Waveform Decompositions

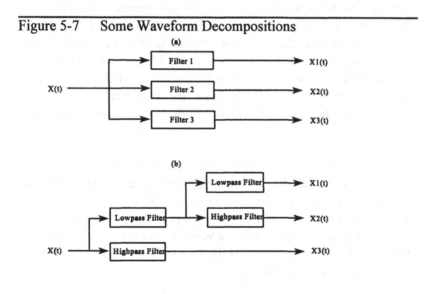

Fast Fourier Transform

The fast Fourier transform (FFT) is an efficient implementation of the discrete Fourier transform (DFT), which is defined as follows:

$$A(k) = \sum x(n) * W^{nk} \qquad \text{for n = 0 to M-1,} \quad \text{/* DFT */}$$
$$x(n) = (\sum A(k) * W^{-nk})/M \quad \text{for k=0 to M-1,} \quad \text{/* Inverse DFT */}$$

where $A(k)$ = amplitude for the k-th harmonic component,
        $x(n)$ = signal value sampled at time n, and
        $W^{nk} = \exp(-j2\pi nk/M) = \cos(2\pi nk/M) - j * \sin(2\pi nk/M)$

DFT basically decomposes a sampled signal into M number of harmonic components. Originally, a signal is continuous. An A/D converter must be used to sample the signal at a fixed time interval to get a digital representation of the signal. Let R be the sampling rate measured in the number of samples per second. In the above DFT formula, M is the number of sampled data the DFT is applied on. This means that there is a window that is M/R seconds long, and the DFT is applied only to the sampled data falling within this window. Let $T = M/R$, which denotes the time period for a cycle of the fundamental frequency. Therefore, the fundamental frequency is 1/T, or R/M, and thus the frequency of the k-th harmonic component is (k*R)/M.

To use FFT, M must be a power of 2. FFT reduces the redundant computations in the DFT formula. A detailed discussion of FFT can be found in [Crenshaw 1995, Atkins and Margulis 1990, Dearman 1995]. Many commercial FFT software products are available. When using an FFT subroutine, a vector (array) of $x(0),...,x(M-1)$ is inputted. After the execution of the FFT subroutine, an output vector of $A(0),...,A(M-1)$ is obtained.

In Figure 5-7, if the bandpass filters are implemented in hardware, the output of each filter can be sampled at a fixed time interval to get data for $x1(n)$, $x2(n)$ and $x3(n)$ in each frame. These sampled data can be used as the features of the frame. However, to implement the bandpass filters in software, $x(n)$ is sampled first, and then FFT is applied to a vector of x(0),...,x(M-1) in each frame. After that, the amplitude for each bandpass filter is obtained by computing the mean square root of those A(n) whose corresponding frequencies fall within the frequency interval of the bandpass filter.

Filtering

Filtering removes unwanted parts of a signal and enhances the good parts. For example, as in Figure 5-7, x(t) may contain high frequency noises. Therefore, before applying FFT or other feature extracting algorithms, it helps to eliminate the noises first.

Filtering can be performed in the frequency or time domain. In the former approach, FFT is used to get A(0),...,A(M), and then each A(n) is multiplied with a filter coefficient f(n). To boost or cut a particular frequency, the value of f(n) is adjusted. For example, when working with music, 3 dB is a factor of two, so multiplying an amplitude by 16 will boost that frequency by 12 dB, and dividing an amplitude by 4 will cut that frequency by 6 dB.

Normally, when designing a filter, a shape is drawn as shown in Figure 5-8, and then f(n) is obtained from the shape. Filtering is performed by computing A'(n)=A(n)*f(n) for n=0,...,M-1. The filtered signal is computed by taking the inverse DFT/FFT on A'(n) for n=0,...,M-1. For a very intuitive discussion of filtering, consult [Lawrence 1991, Crenshaw 1996].

In the time domain approach, formulas are used to compute filtered outputs in a Finite Impulse Response (FIR) filter or Infinite Impulse Response (IIR) filter. The formula for an FIR filter is a weighted sum of the last m sampled signal values as defined below:

$$y(n) = \sum c(n-k)*x(n-k) \quad \text{for } k=0,...,m-1.$$

A special case of the FIR filter is the moving average of x given by

$$y(n) = (\sum x(n-k))/m \quad \text{for } k=0,...,m-1.$$

The formula for an IIR filter is a weighted sum of the last m sampled signal values plus a weighted sum of the last m-1 filtered outputs as given below:

$$y(n) = c(n)*x(n) + \Sigma\, c(n-k)*x(n-k) + \Sigma\, d(n-k)*y(n-k)$$
$$\text{for } k=1,...,m-1.$$

This filter includes feedback. This means that the previous outputs from the filter are fed back into the filter to help determine the next output. A typical IIR filter will be between the second and eighth order, i.e., m is between 2 and 8. However, a typical FIR filter will have m greater than 20.

Figure 5-8   Some common types of filters

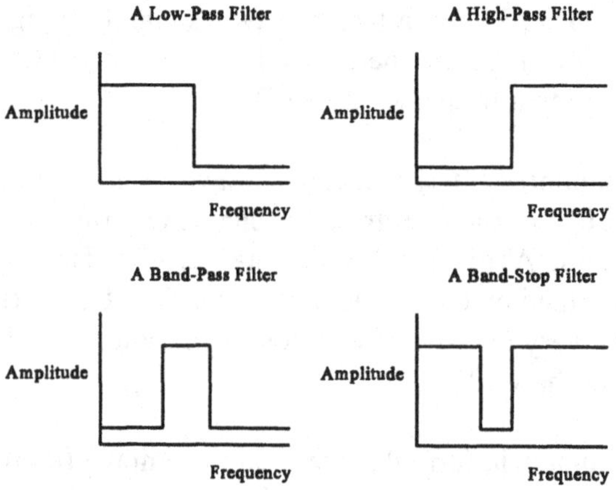

Speech Recognition

Speech recognition has been an important and difficult topic in telephone communication, man-machine interface, and artificial intelligence for over three decades. Due to the tremendous performance improvements of personal computers, there are now several commercial speech recognition software available for a PC platform with a sound or voice card. For example, a voice input point-of-sale (POS) system at a supermarket allows an inexperienced cashier to "say" the name of any non-scannable item such as "banana" rather than looking it up in a book. As speech recognition technology improves further, there will be many more voice-based applications such as voice input and voice output information systems, automatic telephone operators, voice command and telephone dialing in a car, voice-based person identification, and voice-based word processing in the future.

Many techniques and methods such as hidden Markov models [Merlo et al. 1986, Rabiner et al. 1983], neural networks [Palakal and Zoran 1991], speech spectrograms [Johannson et al. 1983, Palakal and Zoran 1991, Stern et al. 1986, Zue and Lamel 1986], Bayesian estimation, dynamic programming, and nearest neighbors have been used for speech recognition. Recently, there have been several proposals that use fuzzy logic for voice-related applications [Hale and Nguyen 1994, Pfister 1995].

Speech can be broken down into two major categories: voiced and unvoiced sounds, corresponding roughly to vowels and consonants respectively. Voiced sounds are quasi-periodic, highly energetic, have more low-frequency than high-frequency energy, and are usually of longer duration than unvoiced sounds. Unvoiced sounds are generally the exact opposite: They are noise-like (not periodic), lower in energy, spectrally flatter, and of shorter duration. The frequency range of speech waveforms is generally from 0 to 3000 Hz.

A speech recognition system usually performs the filtering, segmentation, feature extraction, and classification operations. A

FIR filter can be used to eliminate high-frequency noises. Then, a filtered speech waveform can be divided into frames, where each frame has a time duration between 10 milliseconds (ms) and 20 ms. Note that the vocal tract changes slowly, and is almost stational over intervals of 10 to 20 ms. Each frame has to be labeled by the class or classes it belongs to. Once frames are classified, they can be merged into larger segments.

To tackle the classification problem, each frame will first be classified into either a voiced or unvoiced sound, and then a voiced sound will be classified into a vowel. For the former, the fuzzy program as shown in Figure 5-9 may be used, where the input vairables are the zero crossing and energy of the frame.

Figure 5-9   A Fuzzy Program for Classifying Voiced and
Unvoiced Sounds

```
/* voice.nl */
/*
Copyright © 1996 by Nicesoft Corporation
*/

/*
zc=zero crossing in a frame;
ener=energy of the waveform in a frame;
voi=voiced sound;
unv=unvoiced sound;
nov=no sound, i.e., silent;
*/

membership pack_1(x;a,b,c,d,e,f,g,h)
{
    define low by trapezoid(0,0,a,b);
    define medium by triangle(c,d,e);
    define high by trapezoid(f,g,h,h);
}
```

```
procedure classify(zc,ener; voi,unv,nov;
                   a1,b1,c1,d1,e1,f1,g1,h1,
                   a2,b2,c2,d2,e2,f2,g2,h2,
                   a3,b3,c3,d3,e3,f3,g3,h3)


{
    use pack_1(zc;a1,b1,c1,d1,e1,f1,g1,h1);
    use pack_1(ener;a2,b2,c2,d2,e2,f2,g2,h2);
    use pack_1(voi;a3,b3,c3,d3,e3,f3,g3,h3);
    use pack_1(unv;a3,b3,c3,d3,e3,f3,g3,h3);
    use pack_1(nov;a3,b3,c3,d3,e3,f3,g3,h3);

    if zc is low and ener is high then voi is high;
    if zc is low and ener is medium then voi is medium;

    if zc is high then unv is high;
    if zc is medium and ener is low then unv is high;

    if zc is low and ener is low then nov is high;
}
```

To classify voiced frames, prototypes or templates of the vowel sounds are collected. Then, the waveform in a frame is matched with the stored prototypes. The distances and/or correlations between the waveform and the stored prototypes can be used as the features of the frame. Since there are variations in talking rate, voice volume and voice pitch, time alignment, amplitude normalization and pitch normalization need to be applied to the waveform and prototypes. The method in [Wang et al. 1995] can be used to compute the pitch of a waveform, which is then normalized to a standard value. The formulas for computing a distance, *dis,* or correlation, *cor,* between waveform x and prototype p are given as follows:

$$dis(n) = \Sigma \; abs(x(k) - p(n+k)) \qquad \text{for } k=0,...,M\text{-}1,$$
$$cor(n) = \Sigma \; x(k) * p(n+k) \qquad \text{for } k=0,...,M\text{-}1.$$

The minimum of dis(n), or the maximum of cor(n) will be used as a feature value.

Many prototypes of a specific vowel can be collected to cover many different speakers. For example, Figure 5-10 shows a fuzzy program to classify a waveform into vowel "a" or "u," using one prototype of "a" and two prototypes of "u."

Figure 5-10   A Fuzzy Program for Classifying Vowel "a" or "u"

```
/* vowel.nl */
/*
Copyright © 1996 by Nicesoft Corporation
*/

/*
ad1=distance between waveform and prototype 1 of vowel "a";
ac1=correlation between waveform and prototype 1 of vowel "a";
ud1=distance between waveform and prototype 1 of vowel "u";
ud2=distance between waveform and prototype 2 of vowel "u";
vowa=vowel "a";
vowu=vowel "u";
*/

membership pack_1(x;a,b,c,d,e,f,g,h)
{
    define low by trapezoid(0,0,a,b);
    define medium by triangle(c,d,e);
    define high by trapezoid(f,g,h,h);
}

procedure vowel(ad1,ac1,ud1,ud2;
                vowa,vowu;
                a1,b1,c1,d1,e1,f1,g1,h1,
                a2,b2,c2,d2,e2,f2,g2,h2,
                a3,b3,c3,d3,e3,f3,g3,h3)
```

```
{
    use pack_1(ad1;a1,b1,c1,d1,e1,f1,g1,h1);
    use pack_1(ac1;a2,b2,c2,d2,e2,f2,g2,h2);
    use pack_1(ud1;a1,b1,c1,d1,e1,f1,g1,h1);
    use pack_1(ud2;a1,b1,c1,d1,e1,f1,g1,h1);
    use pack_1(vowa;a3,b3,c3,d3,e3,f3,g3,h3);
    use pack_1(vowu;a3,b3,c3,d3,e3,f3,g3,h3);

    if ad1 is low then vowa is high;
    if ac1 is high then vowa is high;

    if ud1 is low then vowu is high;
    if ud2 is low then vowu is high;
}
```

Machine Tool Breakage Detection

In the manufacturing process that requires the use of mechanical machine tools for metal cutting, drilling, and milling, tool breakage is always a major problem because it can result in defective workpieces or damage to the machine tools. The conventional approach for preventing tool breakage is to maintain the machine tools regularly at a fixed time interval. This approach is not too efficient because the maintenance may be too early or too late due to the large variation in tool life. A better approach is to build a system that constantly monitors the machine tools and detects the right time when they should be maintained, repaired, reconditioned, or replaced.

A mechanical machine tool always makes sounds when it operates. An experienced worker can tell the state of the machine tool by listening to its sounds. For example, a new gear will make different sounds from a worn-out gear. In this section, an acoustic approach will be used to measure, analyze, and classify the state of a machine. It has been shown in [Chen 1994] that fuzzy logic can be used to tackle this problem.

Sounds emitted from a machine tool are recorded via a microphone and a data acquisition board. Even in normal conditions, the sounds may be different due to variations in the machine's rotational speed, the feed rate of a cutting tool, and the workpiece's material. Therefore, data should be collected for many normal operational conditions, and then used as normal prototypes. Sounds can then be compared to the prototypes to see whether they are normal or abnormal. The comparison can be done on the sampled data or on their features. Figure 5-11 shows a fuzzy program based on this general method.

Figure 5-11   A Fuzzy Program for Classifying Machine Sounds

```
/* machine.nl */
/*
Copyright © 1996 by Nicesoft Corporation
*/

/*
d1=distance between waveform and normal prototype 1;
d2=distance between waveform and normal prototype 2;
d3=distance between waveform and normal prototype 3;
normal=normal machine tool;
*/

membership pack_1(x;a,b,c,d,e,f,g,h)
{
    define low by trapezoid(0,0,a,b);
    define medium by triangle(c,d,e);
    define high by trapezoid(f,g,h,h);
}
```

```
procedure machine(d1,d2,d3;
                normal;
                a1,b1,c1,d1,e1,f1,g1,h1,
                a2,b2,c2,d2,e2,f2,g2,h2)
{

    use pack_1(d1;a1,b1,c1,d1,e1,f1,g1,h1);
    use pack_1(d2;a1,b1,c1,d1,e1,f1,g1,h1);
    use pack_1(d3;a1,b1,c1,d1,e1,f1,g1,h1);
    use pack_1(normal;a2,b2,c2,d2,e2,f2,g2,h2);

    if d1 is low then normal is high;
    if d2 is low then normal is high;
    if d3 is low then normal is high;

}
```

Classification of Underwater Acoustic Contacts

The contact classification problem was given in [Leonetti 1994]. Via signal analysis of acoustic sensor data, the objective is to know not only the location, course, and speed of all underwater contacts, but also the indication of what threat, if any, these contacts pose. By classifying a contact and using previously acquired knowledge about the capabilities of that class of contact, one can make intelligent operational decisions.

The approach taken in [Leonetti 1994] is to predict from the signal analysis the number of shafts, number of blades, narrow band acoustic signature, and transient acoustic signature a ship has. Once the information has been gathered, it can be compared to the characteristics of any of the 45 known ship classes reported in [Jordan and Miller 1987, Miller 1989].

To perform the signal analysis, the fast Fourier transform (FFT) is applied to the acoustic waveform at a regular interval. The frequencies whose energies are high are traced over time to get a spectrogram. By analyzing the rate of modulation, as well as the overall frequencies displayed in the spectrogram, the shaft rate and the brade rate can be predicted. They are then used to estimate the number of shafts (1 - 3), and the number of blades (4 - 8). Generally, higher shaft rates at a particular contact speed correlate to a smaller number of shafts.

To get the narrow band acoustic signature and the transient acoustic signature, a library of spectrograms collected for many speed, range and bearing combinations for the known ship classes is needed. By matching a spectrogram with ones in the library, it is possible to get the signature information.

The general approach to this problem has been outlined. The details can only be worked out if you have access to the necessary data.

References

Atkins, M., and Margulis, N. [1990] "Butterflies and FFTs," *Embedded Systems Programming*, May 1990, pp. 26-42.

Chen, J. [1994] "FSC system for tool breakage detection in end milling operations," *Proceedings of the 1994 North American Fuzzy Information Processing Society Conference*, IEEE Catalog Number 94TH8006, pp. 132-135, IEEE Service Center, 445 Hoes Lane, Box 1331, Piscataway, NJ 08855-1331, Tel. 800-678-4333, 908-981-0060, Fax 908-981-1721.

Chen, Y.C., and Chang, P.L. [1995] "An application of fuzzy set approach to the determination of air pollution index," *Proceedings of the 1995 CFSA/IFIS/SOFT International Joint Conference on Fuzzy Theory and Applications*, pp. 332-336, (ed. Weiling Chiang & Jonathan Lee), ISBN 981-02-2485-0, World Scientific Publishing Co., P.O. Box 128, Farrer Road, Singapore 912805.

Cios, K.J., Shin, I., and Goodenday, L.S. [1991] "Using fuzzy sets to diagnose coronary artery stenosis," *IEEE Computer*, March 1991, pp. 57-63.

Corbin, J. [1994] "A fuzzy-logic-based financial transaction system," *Embedded Systems Programming*, December 1994, pp. 24-29.

Crenshaw, J.W. [1994] "The alphabet from S to Z," *Embedded Systems Programming*, August 1994, pp. 60-73.

Crenshaw, J.W. [1994] "The alphabet from S to Z, Part II," *Embedded Systems Programming*, September 1994, pp.64-88.

Crenshaw, J.W. [1995] "All about Fourier Analysis, Part IV," *Embedded Systems Programming*, April 1995, pp. 78-100.

Crenshaw, J.W. [1996] "More on averages," *Embedded Systems Programming*, April 1996, pp. 15-30.

Dearman, C. [1995] "The practical FFT," *Embedded Systems Programming*, May 1995, pp. 28-40.

Hale, C., and Nguyen, C.Q. [1994] "Using fuzzy logic based digital filters for voice command recognition," *Proceedings of Fuzzy Logic'94*, Computer Design, PennWell Publishing Company, Ten Tara Blvd, Nashua, NH 03062-2801.

Hunt, W.F., Ott, W.R., Moran, J., Smith, R., Thom, G., Berg, N., and Korb, B. [1976] "Guideline for public reporting of daily air quality — Pollutant Standards Index (PSI)," U.S. Environment Protection Agency, Research Triangle Park, NC.

Johannson, J., MacAllister, J., Michalek, T., and Ross, S. [1983] "A speech spectrogram expert," *Proceedings of IEEE International Conference on Acoustic, Speech and Signal Processing*, Boston, MA, pp. 746-749.

Jordan, J., and Miller, D. [1987] *Modern Submarine Warfare*, Military Press, Crown Publishers, New York, 1987.

Lawrence, M. [1991] "Son of DSP primer," *Embedded Systems Programming*, November 1991, pp. 65-76.

Leonetti, M.C. [1994] "Classification of underwater acoustic contacts using fuzzy sets," *Proceedings of Fuzzy Logic'94*, Computer Design, PennWell Publishing Company, Ten Tara Blvd, Nashua, NH 03062-2801.

Merlo, E., DeMori, R., Palakal, M., and Mercier, G. [1986] "A continuous parameter and frequency domain based Markov model," *Proceedings of IEEE International Conference on Acoustic, Speech and Signal Processing*, Tokyo.

Miller, D. [1989] *Modern Submarines*, Prentice Hall, New York, 1989.

Morgan, D. [1996] "Multiresolution signal analysis and wavelet decomposition", *Embedded Systems Programming*, July 1996, pp. 30-48.

Nicesoft Corporation [1994] *Decision Plus* — A Fuzzy-Logic-Based Programming Tool, Nicesoft Corporation, 9215 Ashton Ridge, Austin, TX 78750, U.S.A., (512) 331-9027, Fax (512) 219-5837.

Ott, W.R. [1978] *Environmental Indices: Theory and Practice*, Ann Arbor Science.

Palakal, M.J., and Zoran, M.J. [1991] "A neural network-based learning system for speech processing", *Expert Systems With Applications*, Vol. 2, pp. 59-71, 1991.

Pfister, H. [1995] "Fuzzy logic in speech recognition", *Proceedings of Fuzzy Logic'95*, Computer Design, PennWell Publishing Company, Ten Tara Blvd, Nashua, NH 03062-2801.

Rabiner, L.R., Levinson, S.E., and Sondhi, M.M. [1983] "On the application of vector quantization and hidden Markov models to speaker independent isolated word recognition", *Bell Systems Technical Journal*, Vol. 62, pp. 1075-1105.

Rocha, A.F., Morooka, C.K., and Alegre, L. [1996] "Smart oil recovery", *IEEE Spectrum*, July 1996, pp.48-51.

Stern, P.E., Eskenazi, M., and Memmi, D. [1986] "An expert system for speech spectrogram reading", *Proceedings of IEEE International Conference on Acoustic, Speech and Signal Processing*, Tokyo, pp. 1193-1196.

Wang, H.C., Wu, Y.D., Tsukamoto, M., and Inoue, K. [1995] "A method of pitch extraction by fuzzy matching", *Proceedings of the 1995 CFSA/IFIS/SOFT International Joint Conference on Fuzzy Theory and Applications*, pp. 332-336, (ed. Weiling Chiang & Jonathan Lee), ISBN 981-02-2485-0, World Scientific Publishing Co., P.O. Box 128, Farrer Road, Singapore 912805.

Zue, V.W., and Lamel, L.F. [1986] "An expert spectrogram reader: A knowledge-based approach to speech recognition", *Proceedings of IEEE International Conference on Acoustic, Speech and Signal Processing*, Tokyo, pp. 1197-1200.

Chapter 6 Image Analysis

An image is a 2-dimensional representation of objects captured from input devices such as video cameras, VCRs, document scanners, fax machines, film scanners, CCD video microscopes, X-ray machines, magnetic resonance scanners, infrared ray sensors, satellite remote sensors, etc. Mathematically, an image can be thought of as a matrix whose elements are called *pixels*. Each pixel can have a value that represents a gray level or a color at the pixel position.

Images are data. They represent a vast source of information. As the price of a digital still and full-motion video camera or a document scanner drops to a few hundred dollars, more image-based applications will be developed.

An image contains components such as lines, edges, and regions of similar pixels. In the following sections, methods for finding and labeling these components will be described.

Imaging Software Toolkits

When an image is captured into a computer, it is represented by a file. There are many different file formats, including JPEG, CMP, BMP, TIFF, and PCX. Many commercial imaging software tools are available that can be used to perform operations such as scanning, color conversion, display, annotation, processing, file format conversion, compression, and printing on an image file. When purchasing an imaging toolkit, make sure that it supports the file format(s) used by your input device.

An imaging toolkit may be packaged as an OLE Control (OCX), a Visual Basic eXtension (VBX) or a Dynamic Link Library (DLL). An OCX and a VBX package respectively provide OLE and VB controls with properties and methods. To use any of these tools, make sure that the programming language such as Visual C++ 4.0, Visual Basic, Powersoft's PowerBuilder 5.0, or Borland's Delphi 2.0

that are used for developing applications are OCX, VBX, or DDL compliant. Below is a brief description of a few commercial imaging toolkits.

LEADTOOLS

LEADTOOLS is manufactured by Lead Technologies Inc, 900 Baxter Street, Charlotte, NC 28204, USA, Phone 800-637-1853, 704-332-5532, Fax 704-372-8161. It provides various functions for scanning, color conversion, display, annotation, processing, file format conversion, compression, and printing. Its image processing functions include resize, interpolated resize, rotate, flip, invert, reverse, crop, transpose, fill, sharpen, blur, brighten, darken, hue & saturation, intensity detect, stretch intensity, contrast, gamma correct, histogram equalize, edge detect, line detect, mosaic, shear, posterize, median & noise filter, spatial filter (gradient, laplacian, sobel, prewitt, shift & difference, line segment), underlay, region processing, etc. These functions can be used to find components in an image, and to write codes to compute features (e.g., areas, lengths, locations, etc) of the components. The features can be used as inputs to a fuzzy program. The prices of LEADTOOLS packages range from $295 to $1,995. LEADTOOLS DLL functions are listed in Appendix H.

SigmaScan and SigmaScan Pro

SigmaScan and SigmaScan Pro are products made by Jandel Scientific Software, 2591 Kerner Blvd., San Rafael, CA 94901, USA, Phone 800-452-6335, 415-453-6700, Fax 415-453-7782. SigmaScan is used to open digitized images (in TIFF, TGA, PCX, BMP, and JPEG file format) or to scan images with any TWAIN compliant scanner. By directly clicking and drawing lines on or around objects in an image, the image can be measured, using one or more of the 44 manual measurement features such as perimeter, area, shape factor, compactness, number of pixels, center of mass, major/minor axes length, slope, end points, etc. All of the data is stored in the built-in worksheet. These measurement features are especially useful for application areas ranging from life sciences to medical research to materials analysis. SigmScan also provides many other functions for image editing, image processing, image annotation, data analyzing, and data outputing.

SigmaScan Pro supports all of the functions of SigmaScan. In addition, a framegrabber can be used to capture live video images using a CCD camera. It also provides automated measurement features that can be used to count, edge-track, and measure up to 64,000 objects at a time.

GLOBAL LAB Image Development Environment (GLIDE)

GLIDE is made by Data Translation, 100 Locke Drive, Marlboro, MA 01752-1192, USA, Phone 800-525-8528, 508-481-3700, Fax 508-481-8620. GLIDE consists of the GLOBAL LAB Image application program and the GLOBAL LAB Image Processing Library, a Windows DLL of more than 100 image processing and analysis functions. The GLOBAL LAB Image can be used to solve problems in life sciences, medical research, and materials analysis. For example, objects (e.g. cells) in an image can be classified by using size, shape, intensity, position, orientation, or other 51 morphometric measurements. Classes can be defined by pointing out examples of objects belonging to each class. Once a class has been defined, it can be applied to all subsequent images. To develop a custom application, any Microsoft Windows-compatible C Language (Microsoft C, QuickC, or Borland C) can be used with the GLOBAL LAB Image Processing Library. The Library functions are listed in Appendix I.

Imaging For Windows (IFW)

IFW is a product of Wang/Microsoft for Windows 95 and Windows NT 4.0. IFW can be downloaded from one of the following Web sites:
> http://www.windows.microsoft.com
> http://www.wang.com

It will soon be available with every copy of Windows 95 and Windows NT. It supports 32-bit Version 1.6 TWAIN document

scanners only. Images are brought into IFW by scanning, receiving
an inbound fax, importing an existing image file (in TIFF, PCX,
DCX, JPEG, BMP, or AWD format), or by inbound e-mail image
file attachments.

IFW offers OLE Control (OCX) programming interface for Visual
Basic, Delphi and PowerBuilder programmers. By programming
with the IFW's image window, thumbnail, annotation, scanning and
administration OCXs, an image-enable application can easily be
developed.

Edge Detection

An edge is the boundary between two regions with relatively distinct
gray level or color properties. Conventional edge detection
algorithms such as gradient algorithm, Laplacian algorithm and
Sobel's algorithm can be found in [Jain 1989, Gonzalez and Woods
1992].

Figure 6-1   Neighbor pixels of pixel P used for edge detection

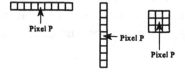

Fuzzy logic has been applied to edge detection [Tyan and Wang 1993, Tao el at. 1993]. The fuzzy logic approach is very flexible because the user can define his/her own fuzzy rules to classify (or assign a membership value to) each pixel of the image, whether it is on an edge or not. A set of fuzzy rules can be designed based on the relationship between each pixel P and its neighbor pixels around P or on a horizontal/vertical line as shown in Figure 6-1.

For each pixel, noises can first be filtered out by taking the average of gray levels or color values of its n neighbor pixels. After filtering, differences of gray levels or color values between pixels are used to detect edges. Figure 6-2 shows a fuzzy program for assigning a membership value to each pixel based on gray levels of its neighbor pixels on a horizontal line. The idea is that if the gray levels are plotted along the pixels on a horizontal line, it will form a curve that is almost flat in a region and has big changes at an edge.

Figure 6-2   A fuzzy program for detecting edge of pixel i

```
/* edge.nl */
/*
Copyright © 1996 by Nicesoft Corporation
*/

/*
left=abs(difference of gray levels between pixel i and pixel i-1);
right=abs(difference of gray levels between pixel i and pixel i+1);
edge=membership value of being on an edge;
*/

membership pack_1(x;a,b,c,d,e,f,g,h)
{
    define low by trapezoid(0,0,a,b);
    define medium by triangle(c,d,e);
    define high by trapezoid(f,g,h,h);
}
```

```
procedure edge(left,right; edge;
                a1,b1,c1,d1,e1,f1,g1,h1,
                a2,b2,c2,d2,e2,f2,g2,h2)
{
    use pack_1(left;a1,b1,c1,d1,e1,f1,g1,h1);
    use pack_1(right;a1,b1,c1,d1,e1,f1,g1,h1);
    use pack_1(edge;a2,b2,c2,d2,e2,f2,g2,h2);

    if left is high and right is low then edge is high;
    if left is low and right is high then edge is high;
    if left is medium and right is low then edge is medium;
    if left is low and right is medium then edge is medium;
}
```

Image Segmentation

A region in an image is a connected area where pixels are similar to each other. In general, a region shows a whole object or a part of it, and can be labeled by the name of the object. The goal of image segmentation is to find regions of the image.

Image segmentation has many applications. For example, as reported in [Jantzen el al. 1993], a physician wants to measure the volume of objects (e.g., brain) inside a patient's head using magneto-resonance (MR) images. The physician gets an MR image on the computer screen and draws out regions of interest using a mouse and a cursor. The computer calculates the area which is then used to calculate the volume of an object. This manual approach is tedious because each patient has 15 slices of MR images, and a typical hospital may have hundreds or thousands of patients. Therefore, it is important to use automated image segmentation.

We shall describe a general fuzzy-logic-based method called the *block matching method* for image segmentation using an MR image of a patient's head as an example. Basically, we shall treat image segmentation as pattern recognition. This method is described as follows: First, the regions of known objects are specified or chosen as classes. Then, each pixel of the image is classified to one of these named regions (classes). For example, in an MR image of the human head, the brain tissue has the light grey region, the fatty tissue has the grey region, and the fluids have the dark grey region. First, the cursor is moved onto each of these regions and is clicked to collect 5x5, 7x7, 9x9 or NxN small blocks of pixels, where N is a small integer. These blocks are used as prototypes of the named regions. For each pixel P of the image, the small block centered at pixel P as shown in Figure 6-1 is chosen. This small block is called the *block* of the pixel P, and is matched with the prototypes. The pixel P is classified to the region of the prototype which has the lowest difference from the block of the pixel P. To match two blocks, the *difference score* is calculated as the sum of the absolute values of the differences of grey levels or color values between the corresponding pixels in the blocks. The difference score may also be calculated by using other matching algorithms. Figure 6-3 shows a fuzzy program for image segmentation based upon the block matching method. After the values of the output variables btr, ftr, and fr are computed by the fuzzy program, the classification of pixel P is computed as follows:

Pixel P is classified to the brain tissue region if btr is highest;
Pixel P is classified to the fatty tissue region if ftr is highest;
Pixel P is classified to the fluids region if fr is highest.

Figure 6-3   A Fuzzy Program for Classifying Pixel P

```
/* segment.nl */
/*
Copyright © 1996 by Nicesoft Corporation
*/

/*
brain1=difference score between the block of pixel P and
     prototype 1 of the brain tissue region;
brain2=difference score between the block of pixel P and
     prototype 2 of the brain tissue region;
```

fat1=difference score between the block of pixel P and
    prototype 1 of the fatty tissue region;
fluid1=difference score between the block of pixel P and
    prototype 1 of the fluids region;
btr=brain tissue region;
ftr=fatty tissue region;
fr=fluids region;
*/

```
membership pack_1(x;a,b,c,d,e,f,g,h)
{
    define low by trapezoid(0,0,a,b);
    define medium by triangle(c,d,e);
    define high by trapezoid(f,g,h,h);
}

procedure segment(brain1,brain2,fat1,fluid1;
            btr,ftr,fr;
            a1,b1,c1,d1,e1,f1,g1,h1,
            a2,b2,c2,d2,e2,f2,g2,h2)
{
    use pack_1(brain1;a1,b1,c1,d1,e1,f1,g1,h1);
    use pack_1(brain2;a1,b1,c1,d1,e1,f1,g1,h1);
    use pack_1(fat1;a1,b1,c1,d1,e1,f1,g1,h1);
    use pack_1(fluid1;a1,b1,c1,d1,e1,f1,g1,h1);
    use pack_1(btr;a2,b2,c2,d2,e2,f2,g2,h2);
    use pack_1(ftr;a2,b2,c2,d2,e2,f2,g2,h2);
    use pack_1(fr;a2,b2,c2,d2,e2,f2,g2,h2);

    if brain1 is low then btr is high;
    if brain2 is low then btr is high;

    if fat1 is low then ftr is high;

    if fluid1 is low then fr is high;
}
```

Image Interpretation

Image interpretation is also called image or scene understanding. The goal is to identify objects and their relationships to each other. In the previous section, the block matching method for image segmentation was introduced, using only the pixel properties of the image. This means that this method transforms an image bitmap to a region bitmap from which regions can be obtained by merging connected pixels that have the same region label. Therefore, this method almost solves the object identification problem. However, there are cases where different objects have similar pixel properties. In these cases, a region may be labeled by more than one name. To tackle this ambiguity, information about relations among regions is used.

In this section, we shall consider finding relations among regions/objects. Finding regions' relations is useful not only for resolving the above described region ambiguity problem, but also for narrating an image. For example, after seeing an image of a natural scene, the computer should be able to say "a red car on a road," "a road across a bridge," "trees beside a road," etc.

The general process flow of image understanding [Miyajima and Ralescu 1993, Krishnapuram and Rhee 1993] is described as follows:

(1) Find image components such as edges and regions from image data.
(2) Compute the components' features such as size and main axis of the regions, inclination and length of the edges, etc.
3) Use the components' features to define and compute the components' relations.

A relation is a proposition such as "a red car on a road." A fuzzy relation is an ill-defined relation. In the real world, many relations of objects in a natural scene are ill-defined. Therefore, it is more appropriate to use fuzzy relations to interpret/understand an image.

Figure 6-4 Regions obtained from image segmentation

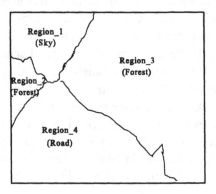

Consider the regions shown in Figure 6-4. The goal is to tell that the
sky (region_1) is above the forest (region_2 and region_3). First, a
fuzzy program is written to define the ill-defined "above" relation
between any two regions R1 and R2. Then, the fuzzy program is
compiled and run. The returned output value of the fuzzy procedure
tells the degree that R1 is above R2. Figure 6-5 shows such a fuzzy
program. The fuzzy program can be tested for the regions shown in
Figure 6-4. The output value should be high for (Region_1,
Region_2), (Region_1, Region_3) and (Region_1, Region_4), but
should be low for (Region_2, Region_3), (Region_2, Region_4) and
(Region_3, Region_4). Note that this fuzzy program works if the
image is taken during the summer when the forest is green. The
fuzzy program can be modified to cover other cases.

Figure 6-5 A fuzzy program for the "above" relation

```
/* above.nl */
/* Copyright © 1996 by Nicesoft Corporation */
/*   miny1=minimum y distance between the top line and R1;
     red1=red value of the color of R1;
     green1=green value of the color of R1;
```

```
    blue1=blue value of the color of R1;
    red2=red value of the color of R2;
    green2=green value of the color of R2;
    blue2=blue value of the color of R2;
    out=output value;   */

membership pack_1(x;a,b,c,d,e,f,g,h)
{
    define low by trapezoid(0,0,a,b);
    define medium by triangle(c,d,e);
    define high by trapezoid(f,g,h,h);
}

procedure above(miny1,red1,green1,blue1,red2,green2,blue2;
                out;
                a1,b1,c1,d1,e1,f1,g1,h1,
                a2,b2,c2,d2,e2,f2,g2,h2,
                a3,b3,c3,d3,e3,f3,g3,h3)

{
    use pack_1(miny1;a1,b1,c1,d1,e1,f1,g1,h1);
    use pack_1(red1;a2,b2,c2,d2,e2,f2,g2,h2);
    use pack_1(green1;a2,b2,c2,d2,e2,f2,g2,h2);
    use pack_1(blue1;a2,b2,c2,d2,e2,f2,g2,h2);
    use pack_1(red2;a2,b2,c2,d2,e2,f2,g2,h2);
    use pack_1(green2;a2,b2,c2,d2,e2,f2,g2,h2);
    use pack_1(blue2;a2,b2,c2,d2,e2,f2,g2,h2);
    use pack_1(out;a3,b3,c3,d3,e3,f3,g3,h3);

    if miny1 is low and
       red1 is low and
       green1 is low and
       blue1 is high and
       red2 is low and
       green2 is high and
       blue2 is low
    then out is high;
}
```

Product Inspection by Machine Vision

Due to the great improvement of performance in hardware and software, machine vision combined with motion control [Babb 1996] has been used intensively in manufacturing applications. By the end of the century, the market could reach $5 billion. In this section, some real-world examples of using machine vision in product inspection [Babb 1996, Davis 1996, Felix and Reddig 1993, Wahl et al. 1983] will be described.

<u>Inspection of Material Cuts</u>

In [Felix and Reddig 1993], the surfaces or cuts of materials are inspected by using an optical device like a microscope or a video camera. A good surface should be uniform and smooth, while a bad one is coarse. The histrograms of pixel gray levels of the images of good and bad surfaces are shown in Figure 6-6.

Figure 6-6   Histograms of good and bad surface images

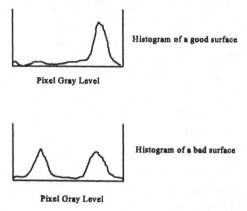

Histogram of a good surface

Pixel Gray Level

Histogram of a bad surface

Pixel Gray Level

Since the good surface tends to have one or a few pixel gray levels, its histogram has only one peak. However, the bad surface is just the opposite. It has many different pixel gray levels, and therefore, its histogram has more than one peak. Given the image of a surface, the histogram of the image can be constructed. Then, the image is classified by matching its histogram with those of the good and bad surfaces. A fuzzy program based on this idea can be easily written.

High-Precision Surface Quality Inspection

In many industries such as magnetic disk and semiconductor wafer manufacturing, surface inspection is always required to detect microscopic surface defects such as voids, cracks, scratches, and asperities. Since these defects have dimensions in the range of only a few micro-inches, a high-precision optical device must be used. In [Wahl el at. 1983], a surface inspection method using an interferometer for detecting the defects was given. In this section, the same problem will be considered to see how fuzzy logic can be used to solve it.

Interferometry is a well-known optical technique that can provide microscopic measurements of a surface. The principle of the interference microscope is shown in Figure 6-7. The incident light beam is split by a beam splitter into two coherent beams with equal intensity. After reflection from equidistant reference and sample surface, the two light beams are recombined by the beam splitter. If the reference mirror is adjusted to have a small wedge angle, the alternate bright and dark interference fringes can be observed in the image plane. The bright and dark fringes are produced by the constructive and destructive waves from the sample and reference beams. The constructive interference occurs when the path difference is an odd multiple of a quarter wave length. The destructive interference occurs at even multiples of a quarter wave length. An interferogram is an image of the interference fringes.

Figure 6-7   Principle of the interference microscope

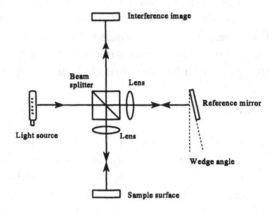

To process an interferogram, the edges between the bright and dark fringes need to be found. As shown in Figure 6-8, the edges for a flat polished surface should be somewhat straight, while for a polished surface that has a small hole, a liquid stain, a long scratch, or a long depression, some of the edges will not be straight. Therefore, by using a fuzzy program to compute the degrees of "straightness" of the fringe lines, the types of defects, e.g., voids, cracks, asperities, on a polished surface can be detected. The automated surface inspection is necessary to avoid inspecting interferograms manually; a time-consuming process, particularly for the microscopic inspections over large areas such as disk surfaces.

Figure 6-8   Fringe lines for various surfaces

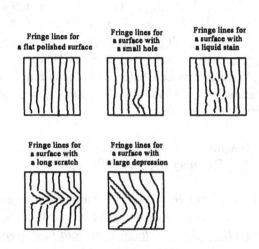

References

Araki, S., Nomura, H., and Wakami, N. [1993] "Segmentation of thermal images using the fuzzy C-means algorithm," *Proceedings of the 2nd IEEE International Conference on Fuzzy Systems,* IEEE Catalog Number 93CH3136-9, pp. 719-724, IEEE Service Center, 445 Hoes Lane, Box 1331, Piscataway, NJ 08855-1331, Tel. 800-678-4333, 908-981-0060, Fax 908-981-1721.

Babb, M. [1996] "Machine vision: High-tech success on the factory floor," *Control Engineering,* July 1996, pp. 65-68.

Bach, J.R., Paul, S., and Jain, R. [1993] "A visual information management system for the interactive retrieval of faces," *IEEE Transactions on Knowledge and Data Engineering,* Vol. 5, No. 4, August 1993, pp. 619-628.

Brown, C. [1994] "Indexing images," *OEM Magazine,* February 1994, pp. 20-23.

Burger, J. [1996] "Mosaics: Emulating the masters," *NewMedia,* June 24, 1996, pp.58-59.

Butterfield, S. [1994] "Process images fast with a real-time OS," *Electronic Design,* April 18, 1994, pp. 73-81.

Child, J. [1996] "Image-processing architectures take new twists," *Computer Design,* July 1996, pp. 53-66.

Cole, B.C. [1994] "Multimedia: Interpreting the standards nightmare," *OEM magazine,* February 1994, pp. 30-44.

Cole, B.C. [1994] "Coming to grips with compression," *OEM Magazine,* April 1994, pp. 28-36.

Davis, A.W. [1995] "Beyond color: The practical world of grayscale imaging, 1995," *Advanced Imaging,* January 1995, pp. 50-53.

Davis, A.W. [1996] "Using machine vision in vision semiconductor wafer inspection," *Advanced Imaging*, June 1996, pp. 56-58.

Eggleston, P. [1995] "Scientific image analysis development tools: Ten common misconceptions corrected," *Advanced Imaging*, October 1995, pp. 48-53.

Felix, R., and Reddig, S. [1993] "Qualitative pattern analysis for industrial quality assurance," *Proceedings of the 2nd IEEE International Conference on Fuzzy Systems*, IEEE Catalog Number 93CH3136-9, pp. 204-206, IEEE Service Center, 445 Hoes Lane, Box 1331, Piscataway, NJ 08855-1331, Tel. 800-678-4333, 908-981-0060, Fax 908-981-1721.

Gardner, D., Andelfinge, R. [1996] "In-air real-time checking for oil debris in aircraft fuel," *Advanced Imaging*, March 1996, pp. 59-61.

Grunin, L. [1992] "Image compression for PC graphics," *PC Magazine*, April 28, 1992, pp. 337-350.

Hamit, F. [1996] "Image database retrieval and sharing: The Getty Art History Information Program," *Advanced Imaging*, March 1996, pp. 42-43.

Jantzen, J., Ring, P., and Christiansen P. [1993] "Image segmentation based on scaled fuzzy membership functions," *Proceedings of the 2nd IEEE International Conference on Fuzzy Systems*, IEEE Catalog Number 93CH3136-9, pp. 714-718, IEEE Service Center, 445 Hoes Lane, Box 1331, Piscataway, NJ 08855-1331, Tel. 800-678-4333, 908-981-0060, Fax 908-981-1721.

Keller, J.M., Chen, Z. [1994] "Image segmentation via fuzzy additive hybrid networks," *Proceedings of the 1994 North American Fuzzy Information Processing Society Conference*, IEEE Catalog Number 94TH8006, pp. 132-135, IEEE Service Center, 445 Hoes Lane, Box 1331, Piscataway, NJ

08855-1331, Tel. 800-678-4333, 908-981-0060,
Fax 908-981-1721.

Krishnapuram, R., and Rhee, F.C.H. [1993] "Compact fuzzy rule
base generation methods for computer vision,"
*Proceedings of the 2nd IEEE International Conference on
Fuzzy Systems*, IEEE Catalog Number 93CH3136-9,
pp. 809-814, IEEE Service Center, 445 Hoes Lane, Box
1331, Piscataway, NJ 08855-1331, Tel. 800-678-4333,
908-981-0060, Fax 908-981-1721.

Kulkarni, A.D. [1995] "Neural-fuzzy decision systems for
multispectral image analysis," *Proceedings of Fuzzy
Logic'95*, Computer Design, PennWell Publishing Company,
Ten Tara Blvd, Nashua, NH 03062-2801.

Loris, K. [1995] "From OCR to document recognition," *Advanced
Imaging*, February 1995, pp. 14-18.

Mantelman, L. [1996] "Get your free imaging software," *Imaging
Magazine*, April 1996, pp.128-140.

Miyajima, K., and Ralescu, A. [1993] "Modeling of natural
objects including fuzziness and application to image
understanding," *Proceedings of the 2nd IEEE International
Conference on Fuzzy Systems*, IEEE Catalog Number
93CH3136-9, pp. 1049-1054, IEEE Service Center, 445 Hoes
Lane, Box 1331, Piscataway, NJ 08855-1331,
Tel. 800-678-4333, 908-981-0060, Fax 908-981-1721.

Moisan, S. [1996] "Grayscale for document capture and
recognition," *Advanced Imaging*, March 1996, pp. 55-58.

Nelson, L.J. [1996] "Commercializing face recognition," *Advanced
Imaging*, March 1996, pp. 85-86.

Okon, C. [1995] "Toward a common video database retrieval
language," *Advanced Imaging*, January 1995, pp. 30-34.

Oomoto, E., and Tanaka, K. [1993] "OVID: Design and implementation of a video-object database system," *IEEE Transactions on Knowledge and Data Engineering*, Vol. 5, No. 4, August 1993, pp. 629-643.

Pomerleau, D., and Todd, J. [1996] "Rapidly adapting machine vision for automated vehicle steering," *IEEE Expert*, April 1996, pp. 19-27.

Russo, F. [1993] "A new class of fuzzy operators for image processing: Design and implementation," *Proceedings of the 2nd IEEE International Conference on Fuzzy Systems*, IEEE Catalog Number 93CH3136-9, pp. 815-820, IEEE Service Center, 445 Hoes Lane, Box 1331, Piscataway, NJ 08855-1331, Tel. 800-678-4333, 908-981-0060, Fax 908-981-1721.

Simon, B. [1993] "Lossless compression: How it works," *PC Magazine*, June 29, 1993, pp. 305-313.

Tao, C.W., Thompson, W.E., and Taur, J.S. [1993] "A fuzzy if-then approach to edge detection," *Proceedings of the 2nd IEEE International Conference on Fuzzy Systems*, IEEE Catalog Number 93CH3136-9, pp. 1356-1360, IEEE Service Center, 445 Hoes Lane, Box 1331, Piscataway, NJ 08855-1331, Tel. 800-678-4333, 908-981-0060, Fax 908-981-1721.

Tyan, C.Y., and Wang, P.P. [1993] "Image processing — Enhancement, filtering and edge detection using the fuzzy logic approach," *Proceedings of the 2nd IEEE International Conference on Fuzzy Systems*, IEEE Catalog Number 93CH3136-9, pp. 600-605, IEEE Service Center, 445 Hoes Lane, Box 1331, Piscataway, NJ 08855-1331, Tel. 800-678-4333, 908-981-0060, Fax 908-981-1721.

Wahl, F., So, S., and Wong, K. [1983] "A hybrid optical-digital image processing method for surface inspection,"

IBM Journal of Research and Development, Vol. 27, No. 4, July 1983, pp. 376-385.

Zhang, W., and Sugeno, M. [1993] "A fuzzy approach to scene understanding," *Proceedings of the 2nd IEEE International Conference on Fuzzy Systems,* IEEE Catalog Number 93CH3136-9, pp. 564-569, IEEE Service Center, 445 Hoes Lane, Box 1331, Piscataway, NJ 08855-1331, Tel. 800-678-4333, 908-981-0060, Fax 908-981-1721.

Chapter 7   Soft Query Processing

There are formated and unformated data in databases. For example, tables in a relational database are formated data, where a relation is represented by a table whose columns correspond to attributes of the relation, and whose rows correspond to records. Examples of unformated data are text, waveforms, and images.

Relational databases are very popular in the business world because the data are arranged in a simple record format, and the searching engines for the standard query languages, such as Query By Example and SQL, are very efficient for processing a large number of records. However, the existing relational databases can not handle ill-defined attributes, nor can it process queries containing "soft" conditions such as "old" employees, "big" companies, etc. In this chapter, fuzzy logic will be used to define ill-defined attributes, and to process soft conditions.

In the real world, about 90% of data are in the form of text, waveforms, and images. However, as of today, there still is not a good query language for these unformated data. For text databases, the decades-old keyword search methods are still used. For waveform databases and image databases, there is still no good way to ask questions. In this chapter, some fuzzy logic approaches to these problems will also be covered.

Soft Attributes in Data Modeling

Data modeling in a relational database means defining relations and their attributes. For example, a relation (table) may be called EMPLOYEE, and its attributes (column names) can include NAME, DEPARTMENT, SALARY, and DATE-OF-BIRTH. Data for each employee are entered manually. In addition, some other attributes (e.g., AGE) can be defined in terms of the existing attributes (e.g., DATE-OF-BIRTH). We call these well-defined attributes "hard" attributes. However, there are ill-defined attributes which are also important for decision making. For example, attributes such as "stock price breakout," "applicant/product rating," "sales trend," "market strength," and "economic health" are useful for making decisions. In contrast to the hard attributes, they are called "soft" attributes. In the following, fuzzy programs are used to define the soft attributes.

Consider a fuzzy program that defines the soft attribute "stock price breakout." The fuzzy program will capture the idea that a stock market expert may buy stocks which have been traded in a "narrow" range for "long" time, and which just made a "big" upside move. This strategy statement contains the fuzzy terms "narrow," "long," and "big."

Every day when a stock is traded, the highest, lowest and closing prices for the day can be recorded. They are called high, low, and close, respectively. The number of shares traded (called a volume) and the closing price change from the previous trading day are also recorded. Price data usually listed in newspapers can be stored in a table such as the table STOCK.DB shown in Figure 7-1.

Figure 7-1   Table STOCK.DB for Sample Daily Price Data

	Stock	Date	High	Low	Close	Change	Volume
1	AAA	1/2/87	5.84	5.64	5.70	0.00	12000
2	AAA	1/3/87	5.68	5.55	5.68	- 0.02	10000
3	AAA	1/4/87	5.70	5.60	5.60	- 0.08	11000
4	AAA	1/5/87	5.60	5.50	5.60	0.00	12000
5	AAA	1/6/87	5.70	5.60	5.70	0.10	13000
6	AAA	1/9/87	5.80	5.66	5.78	0.08	14000
7	AAA	1/10/87	5.92	5.84	5.85	0.07	15000
8	AAA	1/11/87	5.88	5.84	5.84	- 0.01	12000
9	AAA	1/12/87	5.96	5.85	5.91	0.07	15000
10	AAA	1/13/87	5.92	5.86	5.91	0.00	13000
11	AAA	1/16/87	5.92	5.86	5.91	0.00	12000
12	AAA	1/17/87	6.00	5.94	5.98	0.07	15000
13	AAA	1/18/87	5.94	5.70	5.74	- 0.24	17000
14	AAA	1/19/87	5.84	5.72	5.80	0.06	16000
15	AAA	1/20/87	5.87	5.76	5.83	0.03	15000

16	AAA	1/23/87	5.86	5.75	5.84	0.01	12000
17	AAA	1/24/87	5.98	5.88	5.88	0.04	13000
18	AAA	1/25/87	6.02	5.92	5.97	0.09	15000
19	AAA	1/26/87	6.00	5.94	5.97	0.00	14000
20	AAA	1/27/87	5.93	5.86	5.92	- 0.05	14000
21	AAA	1/30/87	5.86	5.70	5.78	- 0.14	15000
22	AAA	1/31/87	5.85	5.78	5.78	0.00	14000
23	AAA	2/1/87	5.84	5.75	5.82	0.04	13000
24	AAA	2/2/87	5.86	5.78	5.78	- 0.04	14000
25	AAA	2/3/87	5.88	5.75	5.84	0.06	15000
26	AAA	2/6/87	5.86	5.82	5.83	- 0.01	12000
27	AAA	2/7/87	5.94	5.86	5.90	0.07	15000
28	AAA	2/8/87	5.88	5.84	5.86	- 0.04	14000
29	AAA	2/9/87	5.84	5.82	5.82	- 0.06	13000
30	AAA	2/10/87	5.84	5.72	5.72	- 0.10	12000
31	AAA	2/14/87	5.75	5.68	5.72	0.00	10000
32	AAA	2/15/87	5.84	5.70	5.70	- 0.02	13000
33	AAA	2/16/87	5.72	5.68	5.72	0.02	10000
34	AAA	2/17/87	5.75	5.66	5.75	0.03	12000
35	AAA	2/20/87	5.80	5.70	5.80	0.05	13000
36	AAA	2/21/87	5.80	5.70	5.74	- 0.06	13000
37	AAA	2/22/87	5.76	5.72	5.72	- 0.02	12000
38	AAA	2/23/87	5.82	5.72	5.72	0.00	12000
39	AAA	2/24/87	5.75	5.69	5.71	- 0.01	10000
40	AAA	2/27/87	5.74	5.68	5.68	- 0.03	11000
41	AAA	2/28/87	5.72	5.66	5.70	- 0.02	10000
42	AAA	3/1/87	5.75	5.68	5.70	0.00	11000
43	AAA	3/2/87	5.76	5.70	5.76	0.06	12000
44	AAA	3/3/87	5.86	5.78	5.84	0.08	15000
45	AAA	3/6/87	5.86	5.70	5.84	0.00	14000
46	AAA	3/7/87	5.84	5.78	5.82	- 0.02	13000
47	AAA	3/8/87	5.84	5.80	5.82	0.00	12000
48	AAA	3/9/87	5.86	5.82	5.82	0.00	11000
49	AAA	3/10/87	5.90	5.84	5.90	0.08	12000
50	AAA	3/13/87	5.94	5.82	5.84	- 0.06	12000
51	AAA	3/14/87	5.86	5.82	5.84	0.00	13000
52	AAA	3/15/87	5.86	5.82	5.83	- 0.01	12000
53	AAA	3/16/87	5.86	5.82	5.84	0.01	12000
54	AAA	3/17/87	5.84	5.80	5.83	- 0.01	10000
55	AAA	3/20/87	5.84	5.78	5.80	- 0.03	11000
56	AAA	3/21/87	6.00	5.84	5.99	0.19	20000
57	AAA	3/22/87	6.16	5.99	6.15	0.16	25000
58	AAA	3/23/87	6.24	6.12	6.14	- 0.01	25000
59	AAA	3/24/87	6.20	6.08	6.18	0.04	28000
60	AAA	3/27/87	6.66	6.26	6.48	0.30	32000
61	AAA	3/28/87	6.66	6.50	6.58	0.10	33000
62	AAA	3/29/87	6.65	6.46	6.46	- 0.12	30000
63	AAA	3/30/87	6.60	6.50	6.55	0.09	32000

64	AAA	3/31/87	6.80	6.58	6.61	0.06	33000
65	AAA	4/3/87	6.70	6.54	6.70	0.09	34000
66	AAA	4/4/87	6.94	6.76	6.83	0.13	36000
67	AAA	4/5/87	7.06	6.90	7.02	0.19	40000
68	AAA	4/6/87	6.96	6.86	6.88	- 0.14	36000
69	AAA	4/7/87	7.16	6.90	7.12	0.24	40000
70	AAA	4/10/87	7.34	7.02	7.08	- 0.04	38000
71	AAA	4/11/87	7.22	7.08	7.16	0.08	39000
72	AAA	4/12/87	7.64	7.20	7.59	0.43	45000
73	AAA	4/13/87	7.60	7.42	7.56	- 0.03	40000
74	AAA	4/14/87	7.64	7.42	7.61	0.05	42000
75	AAA	4/18/87	8.10	7.54	8.11	0.50	44000
76	AAA	4/19/87	8.36	8.00	8.20	0.09	50000
77	AAA	4/20/87	8.42	8.10	8.38	0.18	53000
78	AAA	4/21/87	8.88	8.54	8.88	0.50	56000

These data can be plotted in a bar chart as shown in Figure 7-2, where a vertical line represents a day's price range (by drawing from high to low) and a short horizontal line crossing the vertical line represents the closing price of the day. Note that the vertical and horizontal axes denote Price and Date, respectively. Without loss of representability, indexes of the table's records can be used to denote days, and the high, low, and close at day n are denoted by high(n), low(n), and close(n), respectively.

Figure 7-2   The Bar Chart for the Data in Figure 7-1

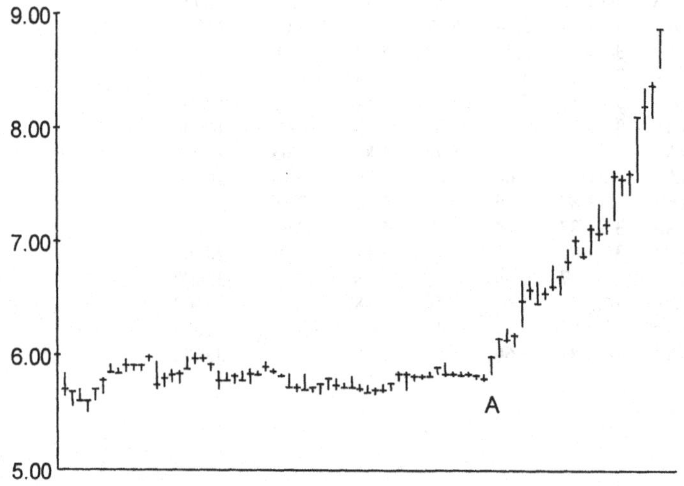

If looking at the bar chart, note that there is an upside price breakout at point A. (For simplicity, this example will focus on upside price breakouts. Downside price breakouts can be treated similarly.) Now, how a breakout is defined so that a program can be written to automatically detect it? The concept of a breakout is certainly fuzzy, and has a degree of truth. In the table of Figure 7-1, a soft attribute for breakout will be added. This means that a breakout will be checked for every day. For any given day, the degree of truth of a breakout depends not only upon the prices of the day but also on the prices of previous days. Therefore, two hard attributes, namely, "duration" and "range," are introduced.

The duration at day n is defined as the maximum number of previous consecutive days whose high's are lower than the close at day n. The concept of duration roughly captures the trading period before the breakout.

The range at day n is defined as the average of the differences between the close prices of all days in the duration at day n and the close price at day n if the duration is not equal to 0. Otherwise, the range is set to 0. The concept of range roughly captures the trading range before the breakout.

Database application programming languages such as Microsoft's Visual Basic for Access, Borland's ObjectPAL for Paradox, or Borland's Delphi for Visual dBase can be used to write a program to compute the values of "duration" and "range" for each day in Figure 7-1. These values are used as inputs to a fuzzy program, shown in Figure 7-3, that computes the value of "breakout" for the day.

Figure 7-3   A Fuzzy Program For Computing Values of Breakout

```
/*
Copyright (C) 1994, 1995 by Nicesoft Corporation
*/
```

```
/*
du=Duration;
r=Range;
b=Breakout;
*/

membership pack_for_duration(x;a,b,c,d,e,f,g)
{
  define short by triangle(0,0,a);
  define medium by triangle(b,c,d);
  define long by trapezoid(e,f,g,g);
}

membership pack_for_range(x;a,b,c,d,e,f,g)
{
  define narrow by triangle(-a,0,a);
  define positive medium by triangle(b,c,d);
  define positive wide by trapezoid(e,f,g,g);
  define negative medium by triangle(-d,-c,-b);
                        /* mirror image of positive medium */
  define negative wide by trapezoid(-g,-g,-f,-e);
                        /* morror image of positive wide    */
}

membership pack_for_breakout(x;a,b,c,d,e,f,g,h)
{
  define small by trapezoid(0,0,a,b);
  define medium by triangle(c,d,e);
  define big by trapezoid(f,g,h,h);
}

procedure breakout(du,r;b;
      a1,b1,c1,d1,e1,f1,g1,
      a2,b2,c2,d2,e2,f2,g2,
      a3,b3,c3,d3,e3,f3,g3,h3)
{
  use pack_for_duration(du;a1,b1,c1,d1,e1,f1,g1);
  use pack_for_range(r;a2,b2,c2,d2,e2,f2,g2);
```

```
use pack_for_breakout(b;a3,b3,c3,d3,e3,f3,g3,h3);

if du is long and r is narrow then b is big;
if du is medium and r is narrow then b is medium;
if du is short then b is small;
if r is positive/medium then b is small;
if r is positive/wide then b is small;
if r is negative/medium then b is small;
if r is negative/wide then b is small;
}
```

The fuzzy program will be compiled into a procedure in a database application programming language such as Visual Basic, ObjectPAL, C with embedded SQL, or Delphi. The fuzzy procedure is tested with the data in Figure 7-1, using the following parameters for the membership functions:

a1	b1	c1	d1	e1	f1	g1
10	0	10	30	20	30	100

a2	b2	c2	d2	e2	f2	g2
0.5	0.2	0.8	1.4	0.5	1.0	3.0

a3	b3	c3	d3	e3	f3	g3	h3
0.1	0.3	0.2	0.4	0.6	0.5	0.8	1.0

Values of the soft attribute "breakout" computed by the fuzzy procedure are shown in the Table in Figure 7-4. Note the breakout on day 56 (3/21/87). The truth of a breakout is 0.82, a high value compared with other values. This breakout day corresponds to the point A shown in Figure 7-2.

Figure 7-4   The Final STOCK.DB Table

	Stock	Date	High	Low	Close	Change	Volume	Duration	range	breakout
1	AAA	1/2/87	5.84	5.64	5.70	0.00	12000	0.00	0.00	0.10
2	AAA	1/3/87	5.68	5.55	5.68	- 0.02	10000	0.00	0.00	0.10
3	AAA	1/4/87	5.70	5.60	5.60	- 0.08	11000	0.00	0.00	0.10
4	AAA	1/5/87	5.60	5.50	5.60	0.00	12000	0.00	0.00	0.10
5	AAA	1/6/87	5.70	5.60	5.70	0.10	13000	3.00	0.07	0.19
6	AAA	1/9/87	5.80	5.66	5.78	0.08	14000	4.00	0.14	0.22
7	AAA	1/10/87	5.92	5.84	5.85	0.07	15000	6.00	0.17	0.28
8	AAA	1/11/87	5.88	5.84	5.84	- 0.01	12000	0.00	0.00	0.10
9	AAA	1/12/87	5.96	5.85	5.91	0.07	15000	1.00	0.07	0.13
10	AAA	1/13/87	5.92	5.86	5.91	0.00	13000	0.00	0.00	0.10
11	AAA	1/16/87	5.92	5.86	5.91	0.00	12000	0.00	0.00	0.10
12	AAA	1/17/87	6.00	5.94	5.98	0.07	15000	11.00	0.21	0.39
13	AAA	1/18/87	5.94	5.70	5.74	- 0.24	17000	0.00	0.00	0.10
14	AAA	1/19/87	5.84	5.72	5.80	0.06	16000	0.00	0.00	0.10
15	AAA	1/20/87	5.87	5.76	5.83	0.03	15000	0.00	0.00	0.10
16	AAA	1/23/87	5.86	5.75	5.84	0.01	12000	0.00	0.00	0.10
17	AAA	1/24/87	5.98	5.88	5.88	0.04	13000	3.00	0.06	0.19
18	AAA	1/25/87	6.02	5.92	5.97	0.09	15000	0.00	0.00	0.10
19	AAA	1/26/87	6.00	5.94	5.97	0.00	14000	0.00	0.00	0.10
20	AAA	1/27/87	5.93	5.86	5.92	- 0.05	14000	0.00	0.00	0.10
21	AAA	1/30/87	5.86	5.70	5.78	- 0.14	15000	0.00	0.00	0.10
22	AAA	1/31/87	5.85	5.78	5.78	0.00	14000	0.00	0.00	0.10
23	AAA	2/1/87	5.84	5.75	5.82	0.04	13000	0.00	0.00	0.10
24	AAA	2/2/87	5.86	5.78	5.78	- 0.04	14000	0.00	0.00	0.10
25	AAA	2/3/87	5.88	5.75	5.84	0.06	15000	0.00	0.00	0.10
26	AAA	2/6/87	5.86	5.82	5.83	- 0.01	12000	0.00	0.00	0.10
27	AAA	2/7/87	5.94	5.86	5.90	0.07	15000	6.00	0.10	0.28
28	AAA	2/8/87	5.88	5.84	5.86	- 0.04	14000	0.00	0.00	0.10
29	AAA	2/9/87	5.84	5.82	5.82	- 0.06	13000	0.00	0.00	0.10
30	AAA	2/10/87	5.84	5.72	5.72	- 0.10	12000	0.00	0.00	0.10
31	AAA	2/14/87	5.75	5.68	5.72	0.00	10000	0.00	0.00	0.10
32	AAA	2/15/87	5.84	5.70	5.70	- 0.02	13000	0.00	0.00	0.10
33	AAA	2/16/87	5.72	5.68	5.72	0.02	10000	0.00	0.00	0.10
34	AAA	2/17/87	5.75	5.66	5.75	0.03	12000	1.00	0.03	0.13
35	AAA	2/20/87	5.80	5.70	5.80	0.05	13000	2.00	0.06	0.16
36	AAA	2/21/87	5.80	5.70	5.74	- 0.06	13000	0.00	0.00	0.10
37	AAA	2/22/87	5.76	5.72	5.72	- 0.02	12000	0.00	0.00	0.10
38	AAA	2/23/87	5.82	5.72	5.72	0.00	12000	0.00	0.00	0.10
39	AAA	2/24/87	5.75	5.69	5.71	- 0.01	10000	0.00	0.00	0.10
40	AAA	2/27/87	5.74	5.68	5.68	- 0.03	11000	0.00	0.00	0.10
41	AAA	2/28/87	5.72	5.66	5.70	- 0.02	10000	0.00	0.00	0.10
42	AAA	3/1/87	5.75	5.68	5.70	0.00	11000	0.00	0.00	0.10
43	AAA	3/2/87	5.76	5.70	5.76	0.06	12000	4.00	0.06	0.22
44	AAA	3/3/87	5.86	5.78	5.84	0.08	15000	15.00	0.11	0.40
45	AAA	3/6/87	5.86	5.70	5.84	0.00	14000	0.00	0.00	0.10
46	AAA	3/7/87	5.84	5.78	5.82	- 0.02	13000	0.00	0.00	0.10
47	AAA	3/8/87	5.84	5.80	5.82	0.00	12000	0.00	0.00	0.10
48	AAA	3/9/87	5.86	5.82	5.82	0.00	11000	0.00	0.00	0.10

49	AAA	3/10/87	5.90	5.84	5.90	0.08	12000	21.00	0.14	0.48
50	AAA	3/13/87	5.94	5.82	5.84	- 0.06	12000	0.00	0.00	0.10
51	AAA	3/14/87	5.86	5.82	5.84	0.00	13000	0.00	0.00	0.10
52	AAA	3/15/87	5.86	5.82	5.83	- 0.01	12000	0.00	0.00	0.10
53	AAA	3/16/87	5.86	5.82	5.84	0.01	12000	0.00	0.00	0.10
54	AAA	3/17/87	5.84	5.80	5.83	- 0.01	10000	0.00	0.00	0.10
55	AAA	3/20/87	5.84	5.78	5.80	- 0.03	11000	0.00	0.00	0.10
56	AAA	3/21/87	6.00	5.84	5.99	0.19	20000	36.00	0.20	0.82
57	AAA	3/22/87	6.16	5.99	6.15	0.16	25000	56.00	0.35	0.50
58	AAA	3/23/87	6.24	6.12	6.14	- 0.01	25000	0.00	0.00	0.10
59	AAA	3/24/87	6.20	6.08	6.18	0.04	28000	0.00	0.00	0.10
60	AAA	3/27/87	6.66	6.26	6.48	0.30	32000	59.00	0.66	0.10
61	AAA	3/28/87	6.66	6.50	6.58	0.10	33000	0.00	0.00	0.10
62	AAA	3/29/87	6.65	6.46	6.46	- 0.12	30000	0.00	0.00	0.10
63	AAA	3/30/87	6.60	6.50	6.55	0.09	32000	0.00	0.00	0.10
64	AAA	3/31/87	6.80	6.58	6.61	0.06	33000	1.00	0.06	0.13
65	AAA	4/3/87	6.70	6.54	6.70	0.09	34000	0.00	0.00	0.10
66	AAA	4/4/87	6.94	6.76	6.83	0.13	36000	65.00	0.94	0.10
67	AAA	4/5/87	7.06	6.90	7.02	0.19	40000	66.00	1.12	0.10
68	AAA	4/6/87	6.96	6.86	6.88	- 0.14	36000	0.00	0.00	0.10
69	AAA	4/7/87	7.16	6.90	7.12	0.24	40000	68.00	1.19	0.10
70	AAA	4/10/87	7.34	7.02	7.08	- 0.04	38000	0.00	0.00	0.10
71	AAA	4/11/87	7.22	7.08	7.16	0.08	39000	0.00	0.00	0.10
72	AAA	4/12/87	7.64	7.20	7.59	0.43	45000	71.00	1.61	0.10
73	AAA	4/13/87	7.60	7.42	7.56	- 0.03	40000	0.00	0.00	0.10
74	AAA	4/14/87	7.64	7.42	7.61	0.05	42000	1.00	0.05	0.13
75	AAA	4/18/87	8.10	7.54	8.11	0.50	44000	74.00	2.06	0.10
76	AAA	4/19/87	8.36	8.00	8.20	0.09	50000	75.00	2.12	0.10
77	AAA	4/20/87	8.42	8.10	8.38	0.18	53000	76.00	2.28	0.10
78	AAA	4/21/87	8.88	8.54	8.88	0.50	56000	77.00	2.75	0.10

Soft Query Representation

Existing relational database systems can only handle queries containing **hard conditions**. For example, "Find suspects whose heights are greater than 5.8 feet" is a query that contains a hard condition "HEIGHT > 5.8." The criterion "5.8 feet" in this case is somehow arbitrarily chosen. This query will not be useful if the real suspect is 5.79 feet tall because a database system will miss him.

A better approach is to allow the user to ask a **soft query** like "Find *tall* suspects." This soft query contains a **soft condition** (HEIGHT is tall). Another soft query is "Find stocks having *high* volume and *big* breakout." Soft queries with soft conditions such as "large" sales, "right" inventory, "severe" infection, "straight" street, "short" distance, "large" object, "dark" area, etc. are convenient for presenting requests to business, health, GIS, and indexed image databases [Chang 1995].

To represent soft queries, the standard SQL can be extended to allow hard as well as soft conditions in the WHERE clause. For example, the following demonstrates an extended SQL statement:

```
SELECT stock
FROM STOCK.DB
WHERE date = today and
        close < 10 and
        volume is high and
        breakout is big.
```

To process this query, the hard and soft conditions in the WHERE clause need to be separated. The following SQL statement whose SELECT clause contains the column names "volume" and "breakout" in the soft conditions "volume is high" and "breakout is big" is generated:

```
        SELECT stock, volume, breakout
        FROM STOCK.DB
        WHERE date = today and
              close < 10.
```

When this SQL statement is passed to a conventional relational database system for execution, you should get the ANSWER table, which has the column names "stock," "volume," and "breakout." Each row in the ANSWER table satisfies the hard conditions "date = today" and "close < 10." Now, the rows in the ANSWER table will be ranked by the soft conditions. This means that the soft conditions are converted into a fuzzy program as shown in Figure 7-5, where "rank" is the soft attribute added to the ANSWER table.

Figure 7-5   A fuzzy program representing the soft conditions
              "volume is high" and "breakout is big"

```
/* Copyright (c) 1994, 1995 by Nicesoft Corporation */

/* answer.db */

/*
v=Volume;
b=Breakout;
r=Rank;
*/

membership pack1(x;a,b,c,d,e,f,g,h)
{
  define low by trapezoid(0,0,a,b);
  define medium by triangle(c,d,e);
  define high by trapezoid(f,g,h,h);
}
```

```
membership pack2(x;a,b,c,d,e,f,g,h)
{
  define small by trapezoid(0,0,a,b);
  define medium by triangle(c,d,e);
  define big by trapezoid(f,g,h,h);
}

procedure rank(v,b;
            r;
            a1,b1,c1,d1,e1,f1,g1,h1,
            a2,b2,c2,d2,e2,f2,g2,h2,
            a3,b3,c3,d3,e3,f3,g3,h3)
{
  use pack1(v;a1,b1,c1,d1,e1,f1,g1,h1);
  use pack2(b;a2,b2,c2,d2,e2,f2,g2,h2);
  use pack1(r;a3,b3,c3,d3,e3,f3,g3,h3);

  if v is high and b is big then r is high;
}
```

This fuzzy program is first compiled into a target language of a database system. Then, for each record of the ANSWER table, the compiled program is called to compute its rank. Once the ranks of all the rows in the ANSWER table are computed, they are sorted in the decreasing order of the rank values. Finally, the user can display/print, say, the top 10 ranked rows.

Complex Queries in Decision Support

A Decision Support System (DSS) on top of a database system (e.g., a data warehouse) must provide answers *quickly* for any query a decision maker may ask. One type of query often asked by him/her is one that compares across dimensions (e.g., time, regions, products, etc). This allows him/her to evaluate the trend and judge the performance. For example, a marketing department may want to compare sales among different products in different regions over different years. A health center may want to analyze distributions of different diseases among different population groups over different periods.

We have surveyed the DSS and its related literature, and found the following examples of queries that should be handled by a DSS system:

> What are the top 10 drug items by geographic region and by season?
> How many trees did we sell at Christmas?
> Give me all product/market combinations for which the net present value of my projected sales for the two years is more than $10 million.
> Did we sell more blue-colored housewares in frostbelt stores this January than we did last January?
> Sales ratio of Alice's products vs. Julie's products.
> Sales percent of Alice's products vs. total products.
> Sales ratio of promoted vs. nonpromoted products.
> Quantity shipped to discount stores vs. department stores.
> Sales of my products to existing vs. new customers.
> Christmas sales this year vs. last year.
> YTD sales this year vs. YTD sales last year.
> How many women over the age of 50, without any previous indications of breast cancer, had a mammogram during the past 12 months in two of the organization's regions and compare the result with the average for all the company's regions.
> Which airline passengers flew to Germany last year and might be

invited to respond to special pricing on tickets for this year?

Which customers bought computers but not printers last month so we can entice them with a discount on a new printer?

Which bank customers with occasional overdrafts and characteristic deposit histories were especially good candidates for home equity loan advertising?

How did Product A sell in the last month, and how does this figure compare to sales in the same month over the last five years? What about by branch, region, and territory?

Did this product sell better in different regions, and are there any regional trends?

Were there more returns of Product A over the last year? Were these returns caused by defects? Were they manufactured in any particular plants?

Do commissions and pricing affect how salespersons sell the product? Do particular salespeople do a better job of selling Product A?

Show sales for the current month and the same month last year for all products that are descendants of the home appliances product line.

Show sales forecast by month for the current year, by quarter for the next year.

Show sales by individual stores and retail chains in California as well as by all retail chains by state.

In order to represent the above queries, the standard SQL language provides aggregate functions AVG, SUM, COUNT, MAX, and MIN so that the user can apply them to groups of records. In the following, the class of queries will be extended by adding a group of members which are characterized by fuzzy logic. For example, consider the query

Show sales of "expensive" products for each store.

Here, "expensive" is a fuzzy term. The conventional approach is to choose an arbitrary cut-point, say $100. This means that if the unit price of a product is greater than $100, it is expensive. Otherwise, it is inexpensive. This approach is not satisfactory because if the price is $99, it is still considered inexpensive. A better approach is to use a fuzzy program as shown in Figure 7-6 to specify the fuzzy term "expensive."

Figure 7-6   A Fuzzy Program for specifying "expensive"

```
* Copyright (c) 1994, 1995 by Nicesoft Corporation */

/* sales.db */

/*
sn=Store Number;
pn=Product Number;
p=Unit Price;
q=Quantity;
a=Amount;
e=Expensive;
*/

membership pack1(x;a,b,c,d,e,f,g,h)
{
  define low by trapezoid(0,0,a,b);
  define medium by triangle(c,d,e);
  define high by trapezoid(f,g,h,h);
}

procedure expense(p;e;
                a1,b1,c1,d1,e1,f1,g1,h1,
                a2,b2,c2,d2,e2,f2,g2,h2)
{
  use pack1(p;a1,b1,c1,d1,e1,f1,g1,h1);
  use pack1(e;a2,b2,c2,d2,e2,f2,g2,h2);

  if p is high then e is high;
  if p is medium then e is medium;
  if p is low then e is low;

}
```

The above fuzzy program is compiled and called to compute the degree of "expensive" for each product. Examples of the results are shown in the following table whose rows have been grouped by Store Number.

Store No.	Product No.	Unit Price	Quantity	Amount	Expensive
s123	p5	150	2	300	1.0
s123	p2	80	1	80	0.7
s123	p3	30	20	600	0.2
s456	p2	80	3	240	0.7
s456	p7	10	100	1000	0.1

To apply COUNT, SUM, MAX, MIN, and AVG to a group, they need to be modified to fuzzyCOUNT, fuzzySUM, fuzzyMAX, fuzzyMIN, and fuzzyAVG, respectively. This means that they are defined for a group G as follows:

> fuzzyCOUNT(A,softA,TH) = SUM of softA(x)
>   for every x in G where softA(x) > TH;
> fuzzySUM(A,softA,TH) = SUM of [A(x)*softA(x)]
>   for every x in G where softA(x) > TH;
> fuzzyMAX(A,softA,TH) = MAX of [A(x)*softA(x)]
>   for every x in G where softA(x) > TH;
> fuzzyMIN(A,softA,TH) = MIN of [A(x)*softA(x)]
>   for every x in G where softA(x) > TH;
> fuzzyAVG(A,softA,TH) = fuzzySUM(A,softA,TH) divided by
>   fuzzyCOUNT(A,softA,TH);

where A is an attribute and softA is a soft attribute of a table, and TH is a threshold value. If x is a member of a group, A(x) and softA(x) denote its attribute and soft attribute value, respectively. Note that a threshold is necessary for preventing low soft attribute values from distorting a final result.

If the fuzzy aggregate functions are applied to store s123, the following is obtained:

$$fuzzyCOUNT(Amount, Expensive, 0.5) = 1.0 + 0.7 = 1.7$$
$$fuzzySUM(Amount, Expensive, 0.5) = 300*1.0 + 80*0.7 = 356$$
$$fuzzyMAX(Amount, Expensive, 0.5) = MAX\{300*1.0, 80*0.7\}$$
$$= 300$$
$$fuzzyMIN(Amount, Expensive, 0.5\} = MIN\{300*1.0, 80*0.7\}$$
$$= 56$$
$$fuzzyAVG(Amount, Expensive, 0.5) = 356/1.7 = 209.41$$

Note that product p3 in this group is not entered into the computation, because its "expensive" score 0.2 is less than the threshold 0.5.

Similarly, the same computation can be applied to store s456. Therefore, the answer to the query is

Store	Sales
s123	356
s456	168

Fuzzy logic is very useful for repesenting queries that have soft conditions. For example, the following queries are very common:

Do teenagers like "dark" colors better than "light" colors?
What is the "recent" top 10 best sellers of "low" price items?
What are "high" volume items that are "new"?

In these queries, the words in quotes are fuzzy terms. By using soft conditions and fuzzy aggregate functions as described above, more interesting and natural queries can be handled. Even though it requires more computer power to process soft queries, it is certainly within the reach of today's computers. Commercial database servers from IBM, ORACLE, SYBASE and INFORMIX employ parallel computing. Very soon soft queries will be processed efficiently.

Geographic Information System (GIS)

A geographic information system [Smith 1996, Wilensky 1996] may contain any of the following geographic data types:

> street and highway maps,
> district, county, and state maps,
> zip code maps,
> telephone area code maps,
> census data distribution maps (e.g., population, income),
> environmental data distribution maps (e.g., air pollution),
> water and soil distribution maps,
> topographic and land use maps,
> weather maps,
> business data distribution maps (e.g., restaurant),
> satellite images,
> digitized aerial photographs.

In addition, the geographic data may be associated with textual materials (e.g, city, airport, highway, farm, river, or mountain names) that describe geographic terms and features. A geographic feature and an associated name (e.g., [city,San Francisco]) in a map is called a *gazetteer*. Most of the queries in a GIS are stated by using the geographic terms and features. You may use the standard terms from the US Machine-Readable Cataloging (USMARC) standard [Library of Congress MARC Development Office 1976] and Federal Geographic Data Committee (FGDC) metadata standards [Federal Geographic Data Committee 1991]. In order to facilitate the efficient executions of the queries, indexes and catalogs for the geographic data must be created.

When building a GIS, many issues need to be considered. The first issue is that, very often, the exact nature of a name in a map is fuzzy. For example, does "San Francisco" mean the city limits, downtown area, or City Hall? An index for "San Francisco" may only give the location of a point in a map. When the GIS displays the San Francisco area, it has to decide how big the area will be displayed. The second issue is that the user may want to refer to an area or place by a fuzzy relation to a known name. e.g., South of San Francisco. The third issue is that even a standard geographic feature itself is not well defined. For example, we may say "populated place" and "developed area." All these issues involve fuzzy concepts. Therefore, the methods described in the previous sections for defining soft attributes and representing soft queries will be useful for building a user-friendly GIS.

Retrieval Methods in Image Databases

Keyword-based and content-based retrieval methods are used in image databases. The former is used in [Bielski 1995, Hamit 1996], while the latter is used in [Bach el al. 1993, Brown 1994, Gupta 1995, Jain 1996, Nelson 1996]. In applications such as product image databases, news photo databases [Bielski 1995], and art museum painting collections [Hamit 1996], images are thoroughly cataloged by descriptive fields, including the caption field for textual descriptions. A query is usually represented by constraints on catalog fields and a set of keywords for the caption. The keyword-based retrieval method searches for images that satisfy the constraints and match the keywords in the captions. This approach is adequate if the user specifies the constraints only on the defined fields and chooses the keywords carefully.

On the other hand, for applications such as face, fingerprint, medical image record, and material microscopic image databases, it is better to use the content-based retieval method. The idea of the content-based retrieval method is to use an image as a query and search an image database to find those images that closely match the query image. The matching is usually based on comparing the features of the images. When an image is inserted into the database, its features are computed and indexes on the features are created. In the query time, the features of the query image are computed and matched with those in the image database. This approach is often called Query By Pictorial Example. A software product named Query By Image Content (QBIC) from IBM [Brown 1994] allows the user to use the features to specify a query.

As to what features of an image should be used for image matching, consider the way human beings approach visual images. When confronted with a new image, human observers first scan for recognizable objects. When they have identified such an object or objects, they then take in the dominant characteristics of these objects, such as shape, color, texture, histogram, and edge direction. Finally, if multiple objects are present, observers take note of the relative positions of the objects.

In order to handle a large image database, images need to be organized and indexed so that a search can be performed efficiently. For example, consider a database of 100,000 face images. It would be time-consuming if the query image is matched with each of them. However, a two-step strategy may circumvent this difficulty by pre-classifying a face according to its "type." Facial types might include characteristics such as race, shape (e.g. oval, round, angular), nose size, and gender. All of the images in the database are classified into type categories, and an index for them is built. When the query image is processed, it is classified into a type category and then matched with images only in the type category of the query image. Since the type category may contain only 100 images, matching is much less time-consuming.

A general description of the computations such as feature-defintion, classification, and matching involved in the content-based search of images has been given. As discussed in Chapter 6, fuzzy logic can be used in all of these computations.

References

Chang, C.L. [1995] "Fuzzy-logic-based query representation in decision support," _Proceedings of Fuzzy Logic'95_, Computer Design, PennWell Publishing Company, Ten Tara Blvd, Nashua, NH 03062-2801.

Decision Support

Appleton, E. [1995] "Support decision makers with a data warehouse," _Datamation_, March 15, 1995, pp.53-58.

Bulos, D. [1995] "How to evaluate OLAP servers," _DBMS_, August 1995, pp.96-103.

Celko, J. [1995] "The world of software," _DBMS_, June 1995, pp.17-20.

Codd, E.F., S.B. Codd, and C.T. Salley [1993] "Providing OLAP to user analysts: An IT Mandate," Codd & Date Inc., 1993.

Ehrmann, D. [1995] "Top X/Bottom Y revisited," _Paradox Informant_, January 1995, pp.38-47.

Finkelstein, R. [1995] "MDD: Database reaches the next dimension," _Database Programming & Design_, April 1995, pp.27-38.

Frank, M. [1995] "The truth about OLAP," _DBMS_, August 1995, pp.40-48.

Grygo, E.M. [1995] "An information warehouse on SMP," _Client/Server Computing_, July 1995, pp.20-26.

Gutkowski, G. [1995] "Tips on teting OLAP servers," _Datamation_, June 1, 1995, pp.9.

Hackathorn, R. [1995] "Data warehousing energizes your
    enterprise," *Datamation*, February 1, 1995, pp.38-43.

Inmon, W., and R. Hackathorn [1994] *Using the Data Warehouse*,
    John Wiley & Sons, 1994.

Kimball, R. [1994] "The doctor of DSS," *DBMS*, July 1994,
    pp.54-81.

Kimball, R. [1996] "Factless fact tables," *DBMS*, September 1996,
    pp. 16-18.

Kimball, R., and K. Strehlo [1994] "Why decision support fails and
    how to fix it," *Datamation*, June 1, 1994, pp.40-45.

Larsen, S. [1995] "Query I/O Parallelism," *Database Programming
    & Design*, March 1995, pp.46-51.

Mayer, J.H. [1995] "The warehouse craze hits IS," *Reseller
    Management*, August 1995, pp.33-36.

Moriarty, T. [1995] "A data warehouse primer," *Database
    Programming & Design*, July 1995, pp.57-59.

Moriarty, T. [1995] "Modeling data warehouses," *Database
    Programming & Design*, August 1995, pp.61-65.

Poe, V. [1995] "Data Warehouse: Architecture is not infrastructure,"
    Database Programming & Design, July 1995, pp.24-31.

Stodder, D., and A. Pucky [1995] "Software AG's data warehouse
    push," *Database Programming & Design*, July 1995,
    pp.68-69.

The, L. [1995] "OLAP answers tough business questions,"
    Datamation, May 1, 1995, pp.65-72.

Weldon, J-L. [1995] "Managing multidimensionl data: Harnessing the power," _Database Programming & Design_, August 1995, pp.24-33.

White, C. [1995] "The key to a data warehouse," _Database Programming & Design_, February 1995, pp.23-25.

Map and Image Databases

Bach, J.R., Paul, S., and Jain. R. [1993] "A visual information management system for the interactive retrieval of faces," _IEEE Transactions on Knowledge and Data Engineering_, Vol. 5, No. 4, August 1993, pp. 619-628.

Bielski, L. [1995] "20 million photos will be digitized at Time Warner: The image database of the future begins," _Advanced Imaging_, October 1995, pp. 26-28.

Brown, C. [1994] "Indexing images," _OEM Magazine_, February 1994, pp. 20-23.

Brown, E. [1994] "Query technology recognizes colors and shapes," _NewMedia_, June 1994, pp. 24.

Carbonell, J. [1996] "Digital librarians: Beyond the digital book stack," _IEEE Expert_, June 1996, pp. 11-13.

Federal Geographic Data Committee (FGDC) [1991] _FGDC Newsletter_, No. 1, Spring 1991, Federal Geographic Data Committee, Reston, Va.

Flynn, J. [1996] "Use the Web for imaging," _Datamation_, June 1, 1996, pp. 62-65.

Gupta, A. [1995] "Visual information retrieval technology," Virage Inc., 9605 Scranton Rd., Suite #240, San Diego, CA 92121, USA.

Hamit, F. [1996] "Image database retrieval and sharing: The Getty
    Art History Information Project," *Advanced Imaging*,
    pp. 42-43.

Jain, R. [1996] "From content-based retrieval to invisible
    telepresence," *Computer*, June 1996, pp. 85-86.

Koller, D., and Shoham, Y. [1996] "Information agents: A new
    challenge for AI," *IEEE Expert*, June 1996, pp. 8-10.

Library of Congress MARC Development Office [1976]
    Maps: A MARC Format, Library of Congress Information
    Systems Office, Washington, D.C., 1976.

Nelson, L.J. [1996] "Commercializing face recognition: How to
    judge fresh players & approaches," *Advanced Imaging*,
    March 1996, pp. 85-86.

Okon, C. [1995] "Media streams: Toward a common video database
    retrieval language," *Advanced Imaging*, January 1995,
    pp. 30-34.

Oomoto, E., and Tanaka, K. [1993] "OVID: Design and
    implementation of a video-object database system,"
    IEEE Transactions on Knowledge and Data Engineering,
    Vol. 5, No. 4, August 1993, pp. 629-643.

Schatz, B., and Chen, H. [1996] "Building large-scale digital
    libraries," *Computer*, May 1996, pp. 22-26.

Schatz, B., Mischo, W.H., Cole, T.W., Hardin, J.B., Bishop, A.P.,
    and Chen, H. [1996] "Federating diverse collections of
    scientific literature," *Computer*, May 1996, pp. 28-36.

Smith, T.R. [1996] "A digital library for geographically referenced
    materials," *Computer*, May 1996, pp. 54-60.

Wactlar, H.D., Kanade, T., Smith, M.A., and Stevens, S.M. [1996] "Intelligent access to digital video: Informedia project," *Computer*, May 1996, pp. 46-52.

Wilensky, R. [1996] "Toward work-centered digital information services," *Computer*, May 1996, pp. 37-44.

Chapter 8   Data Mining

The purpose of data mining is to discover patterns in data. The necessary requiement of data mining is that you have data. Depending upon the application, the size of data can be small or large. For example, if the goal is to find rules for truck docking or car parallel parking, an expert driver may perform this task and data can be collected by sampling the sensor measurements of input and output variables at a fixed time interval. From the collected data, the subsequent algorithms can be applied to generate fuzzy rules. Usually, a data set collected for a control system is small.

Similarly, data can be collected for manufacturing processes. For example, at Bayer [Manji 1996], the manufacturing process in a Dorlastan spandex production plant is quite complex. Dorlastan spandex is a synthetic fiber produced from a segmented polyurethane/polyurea polymer that is spun to form the fiber. The fiber produced is an elastomeric material that is formed in a denier range of 10 to 1120 in a highly automated dry spinning process. The elastomeric polymer is synthesized from the diisocyanate MDI and a diol PTMEG using standard prepolymerization and chain extension steps to form the polymer dissolved in a polar solvent. The resulting polymer solution is then modified with a series of functional additives to yield the desired spin solution. Then, in a dry spinning process, the solvent is driven out of a polymer solution under high temperature in an inert gas loop. The resulting fiber is wound at high speeds at the outlet of the spin duct, while the solvent is recovered for reuse. To monitor this manufacturing process, a system is set up to collect process, production, and quality data at 4000 points. Because the size of data is large, they are stored in a relational database. The process data are used to correlate with laboratory quality tests and production information.

Over the past 15 to 20 years, the business world has been using computers to capture detailed transaction information. Retail sales, telecommunications, banking, and credit card operations are examples of transaction-intensive industries. Due to the great performance improvement in harware and software, high volumes of transaction-based information can be easily and inexpensively captured. When the transaction data are processed and used, they become historical data. The historical data are transfered to and stored in a data warehouse which is often implemented by a parallel relational database. The purpose of the data warehouse is not simply to keep the data in the archives, but to find values in the data. For example, can the data be used to predict the customer buying pattern, the sales trend, or the bad loan pattern? These questions can be answered by using data mining techniques.

Defining Data Mining

Data mining uses discovery-based algorithms to determine the relationships, patterns, and assocations in the data. More specifically in the context of rule-based systems, data mining automatically generates rules for a specific application. For example, you may want to find rules that correctly describe the relationship between the data of some variables and the data of other variables in a control or manufacturing system. This kind of problem is called *data mining for relationship discovery*.

Another example of data mining is when you have data for cases of "bad" loans and you want to find rules that can describe the patterns of these bad loans. This kind of problem is called *data mining for pattern recognition*.

An activity may be a single transaction, or a sequence of transactions charged with the same account number, credit card, or frequent buyer/flyer number within a specified time period. In traditional market-basket analysis [Moxon 1996], data collected for each activity are analyzed to see what items are purchased together and in what sequences. For example, airlines capture data not only on where their customers are flying, but also on the ultimate destination of passengers who change carriers in mid-flight. By using that data, airlines can identify popular locations that they do not service and add routes to gather that business.

ShopKo Stores, a \$2 billion regional discounter, has also discovered that customers who come in to buy one product often buy another associated product, but that many associations are one-way streets. For instance, film does not cause a camera sale, but a camera sale often causes a film sale. *Data mining for association discovery* finds rules to identify customers who purchase associated products.

Discovering Relationships Among Variables

Consider the data shown in the table of Figure 8-1. The goal is to find fuzzy rules that may describe the relationship between variables x1, x2, x3 and variable y.

Figure 8-1   Table of data for variables x1, x2, x3 and y

x1	x2	x3	y
1.2	2.3	10	80
2.0	1.5	60	87
3.2	0.5	97	92
0.7	3.0	50	90
5.6	6.2	54	58
4.8	5.7	12	47
4.2	4.9	92	52
7.8	9.0	80	30
8.5	7.8	86	28
9.0	7.6	91	19
8.2	8.6	79	15

Our approach, which is called the *fuzzy quantification method,* is given as follows, using the data in Figure 8-1 as an example:

STEP 1:   Define fuzzy quantifications for all of the variables in the table.

We define the fuzzy quantifications for variables x1, x2, x3 and y, using the membership functions shown in Figure 8-2.

Figure 8-2   Some specific membership functions

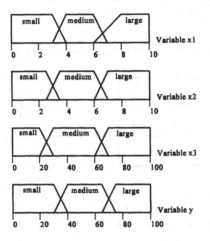

STEP 2:   Replace every numerical value in the table by a fuzzy quantification name.

For example, take the value in column 1 and row 1. The value is 1.2, a value of variable x1. There are 3 fuzzy quantifications, namely, "small," "medium," and "large," for variable x1. The value is replaced by the fuzzy quantification whose membership value is the highest. Using the membership functions in Figure 8-2, the numerical value 1.2 is replaced by "small." This process is repeated for all of the numerical values in Figure 8-1, and the result is the *fuzzy symbol table* shown in Figure 8-3.

Figure 8-3   Table of fuzzy symbol for variables x1, x2, x3 and y

x1	x2	x3	y
small	small	small	large
small	small	medium	large
small	small	large	large
small	small	medium	large
medium	medium	medium	medium
medium	medium	small	medium
medium	medium	large	medium
large	large	large	small
large	large	large	small
large	large	large	small
large	large	large	small

STEP 3:   Consider every row in the fuzzy symbol table as a fuzzy rule, and apply the fuzzy rule minimization to reduce the number of fuzzy rules.

The *fuzzy rule minimization method* is similar to the minimization method [Slagle et al. 1970] used for a switching function in Boolean algebra. The rule minimization for fuzzy logic is also proposed in [Hung and Fernandez 1993]. The idea is to get *fuzzy sum-of-products expressions* from fuzzy rules, and then simplify the fuzzy expressions. Since the variables x1, x2, and x3 are considered as input variables, the variable y as an output variable, and each row in Figure 8-3 as a fuzzy rule, the fuzzy symbol table can be represented by the following fuzzy sum-of-products expressions:

y.large   =   (x1.small)(x2.small)(x3.small) +
                (x1.small)(x2.small)(x3.medium) +
                (x1.small)(x2.small)(x3.large) +
                (x1,small)(x2.small)(x3.medium).

y.medium =   (x1.medium)(x2.medium)(x3.medium) +
                (x1.medium)(x2.medium)(x3.small) +
                (x1.medium)(x2.medium)(x3.large).

y.small   =   (x1.large)(x2.large)(x3.large) +
                (x1.large)(x2.large)(x3.large) +
                (x1.large)(x2.large)(x3.large) +
                (x1.large)(x2.large)(x3.large).

Note that the fuzzy sum-of-products expression is obtained for every fuzzy quantification of the output variable y.

By eliminating the redundant products, the following fuzzy expressions are obtained:

y.large   =   (x1.small)(x2.small)(x3.small) +
                (x1.small)(x2.small)(x3.medium) +
                (x1.small)(x2.small)(x3.large).

y.medium =   (x1.medium)(x2.medium)(x3.medium) +
                (x1.medium)(x2.medium)(x3.small) +
                (x1.medium)(x2.medium)(x3.large).

y.small   =   (x1.large)(x2.large)(x3.large).

By factoring out the common fuzzy expressions, the following fuzzy expressions are obtained:

y.large   =   (x1.small)(x2.small)[x3.small + x3.medium +
                                    x3.large].

y.medium   =   (x1.medium)(x2.medium)[x3.medium +
                                    x3.small + x3.large].

y.small   =   (x1.large)(x2.large)(x3.large).

Because the fuzzy expression [x3.small + x3.medium + x3.large]
covers all of the fuzzy quantifications for x3, it is eliminated, and
the following fuzzy expressions are obtained:

y.large   =   (x1.small)(x2.small).

y.medium   =   (x1.medium)(x2.medium).

y.small   =   (x1.large)(x2.large)(x3.large).

These fuzzy expressions correspond to the following fuzzy rules that
approximately define the relationship between x1, x2, x3 and y:

   if x1 is small and x2 is small then y is large;
   if x1 is medium and x2 is medium then y is medium;
   if x1 is large and x2 is large and x3 is large then y is small;

The fuzzy rule minimization method described above is very
general. It minimizes the number of fuzzy rules. Other minimization
criteria such as the number of products or the number of fuzzy
quantifications in a fuzzy expression can also be used. It is also
possible to introduce intermediate variables for some fuzzy sub-
expressions. For example, consider the following fuzzy expression:

z.large   =   (x1.large)(x2.small)[x3.small + x4.large].

By introducing the intermediate variable y for the fuzzy sub-
expression, [x3.small + x4.large], the following fuzzy expressions
are obtained:

y.high   =   x3.small + x4.large.

z.large   =   (x1.large)(x2.small)(y.high).

These fuzzy expressions correspond to the following fuzzy rules whose network structure is shown in Figure 8-4.

   if x3 is small then y is high;
   if x4 is large then y is high;

   if x1 is large and x2 is small and y is high then z is large;

Figure 8-4   The network structure for variables x1, x2, x3, x4, y, z

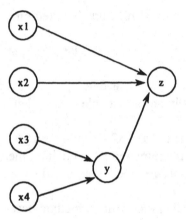

Discovering Rules for Characterizing Classes

For a discovery system to find fuzzy rules automatically for a class, it needs to have data/records of the class. If the records are in a relational database, an SQL query can be entered to retrieve them. For example, over the years, a bank or an insurance company may have kept all of the cases where frauds have been detected. If fuzzy rules can be found to characterize these fraudulent cases, they can be used to detect or prevent frauds in the future. Another example is to find fuzzy rules from the previous examples of "good" and "bad" loans. The fuzzy rules can be used not only to classify whether a loan applicant is a good or bad risk, but also to generate a credit-worthiness "score."

In general, any SQL query can be asked to retrieve records for data mining. The goal is to find fuzzy rules to characterize the class of the retrieved records. For example, a salesman may want to analyze people in New England who have bought pickup trucks. The SQL query defining this class of customers is

SELECT name, age, income, date
FROM customer
WHERE area = New England and
        bought = pickup truck.

By analyzing the records that satisfy this SQL query, the salesman may find out that in winter, people in New England of a certain age group and income level, are likely to buy pickup trucks.

The fuzzy quantification method described in the previous section will be used to find fuzzy rules for characterizing a class. Consider the sales of pen-based Personal Digital Assistants (PDAs) in Japan. These PDAs provide short-distance wireless communications. The following SQL query is used to retrieve the records:

SELECT name, sex, age
FROM customer
WHERE country = Japan and item = FDA.

Assume that the retrieved records are given in Figure 8-5. The goal is to see whether certain patterns can be found in these records. Note that the table in Figure 8-5 is small because the purpose is to use it as an illustration of the fuzzy quantification method.

Figure 8-5   Table of the PDA sales records

name	sex	age
Tanaka	F	14
Hirota	F	17
Hirakawa	F	12
Ishihara	F	15
Nishimori	M	30

The fuzzy quantifications "very_young," "young," "middle_age," "old," and "very_old" are used for the attribute "age." The membership functions are shown in Figure 8-6.

Figgure 8-6   Some specific membership functions

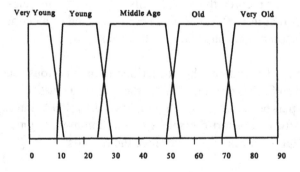

Using the membership functions in Figure 8-6 to replace the ages in Figure 8-5 by the fuzzy quantifications, a fuzzy symbol table as shown in Figure 8-7 is obtained.

Figure 8-7   The fuzzy symbol table for Figure 8-5

name	sex	age
Tanaka	F	young
Hirota	F	young
Hirakawa	F	young
Ishihara	F	young
Nishimori	M	middle_age

Let the class be denoted as FDAsales, which is used as the output variable. Let the fuzzy quantifications for FDAsales be "high," "medium," and "low." Using the rows in Figure 8-7, the following fuzzy sum-of-products expression is obtained:

FDAsales.high   =   (sex.F)(age.young) +
(sex.F)(age.young) +
(sex.F)(age.young) +
(sex.F)(age.young) +
(sex.M)(age.middle_age).

Simplifying the above fuzzy expression, the following is obtained:

FDAsales.high   =   (sex.F)(age.young) +
(sex.M)(age.middle_age).

The fuzzy expression, (sex.F)(age.young), should be weighted more than the fuzzy expression, (sex.M)(age.middle_age), because the former accounts for 80 percent of the cases, while the latter for only 20 percent. Therefore, to *approximately* characterize the class, let

FDAsales.high   =   (sex.F)(age.young),

whose corresponding fuzzy rule is

if sex is F and age is young then FDAsales is high.

This pattern shows that most of the people who buy FDA are young girls. It turns out that the young girls use PDA to send email in classrooms to make comments about their teachers and classmates. A PDA is a very handy tool for a young girl to write a short note in Japanese with an electronic pen.

To classify an object into one of several classes, e.g., good_loan and bad_load, a fuzzy expression is obtained for each class by using the above method. The common sub-expressions that appear in more than one fuzzy expression is then deleted. For example, consider the following fuzzy expressions:

class1.high   =   (x1.small)(x2.large)(x3.high) +
                     (x2.small)(x3.low).

class2.high   =   (x1.large)(x2.small)(x3.low) +
                     (x2.small)(x3.low).

In this case, the sub-expression, (x2.small)(x3.low), should be deleted to obtain

class1.high   =   (x1.small)(x2.large)(x3.high).

class2.high   =   (x1.large)(x2.small)(x3.low).

Using x1, x2, and x3 as input variables, and class1 and class2 as output variables (as described in Chapter 5), a fuzzy program, as shown in Figure 8-8, can be written from the above two fuzzy expressions.

Figure 8-8   A Fuzzy Program for classifying an object

```
/* classify.nl */
/*
Copyright © 1996 by Nicesoft Corporation
*/

/*
x1=The value of the attribute x1 of the object;
x2=The value of the attribute x2 of the object;
x3=The value of the attribute x3 of the object;
class1=Class 1;
class2=Class 2;
*/

membership pack_1(x;a,b,c,d,e,f,g,h)
{
    define small by trapezoid(0,0,a,b);
    define medium by triangle(c,d,e);
    define large by trapezoid(f,g,h,h);
}

membership pack_2(x;a,b,c,d,e,f,g,h)
{
    define low by trapezoid(0,0,a,b);
    define medium by triangle(c,d,e);
    define high by trapezoid(f,g,h,h);
}

procedure classify(x1,x2,x3;
                class1,class2;
                a1,b1,c1,d1,e1,f1,g1,h1,
                a2,b2,c2,d2,e2,f2,g2,h2,
                a3,b3,c3,d3,e3,f3,g3,h3,
                a4,b4,c4,d4,e4,f4,g4,h4)
```

```
{
    use pack_1(x1;a1,b1,c1,d1,e1,f1,g1,h1);
    use pack_1(x2;a2,b2,c2,d2,e2,f2,g2,h2);
    use pack_2(x3;a3,b3,c3,d3,e3,f3,g3,h3);
    use pack_2(class1;a4,b4,c4,d4,e4,f4,g4,h4);
    use pack_2(class2;a4,b4,c4,d4,e4,f4,g4,h4);

    if x1 is small and x2 is large and x3 is high then class1 is high;

    if x1 is large and x2 is small and x3 is low then class2 is high;
}
```

Discovering Data Association

The goal of data association analysis is to find patterns of activities where associated products or services are purchased together. This information can be used to adjust inventories, modify floor or shelf layouts, or introduce a promotional sales campaign to increase overall sales or move specific products.

The approach is to first get a set of records of sales for each product, and then use the intersections of the sets for different products sold. For example, get a set S1 of records satisfying the SQL query

```
SELECT account#, name, age, sex
FROM customer
WHERE purchase_date >= 19960701 and
      purchase_date <= 19960930 and
      purchase_item = beer.
```

Also, get a set S2 of records satisfying another SQL query

```
SELECT account#, name, age, sex
FROM customer
WHERE purchase_date >= 19960701 and
      purchase_date <= 19960930 and
      purchase_item = potato chips.
```

The intersection of S1 and S2 is the set where the same account# appears in both S1 and S2. If the ratio of count(S1 ∩ S2) and count(S1) is large, it means that a large percent of all transactions in which beer was purchased also included potato chips. Note that the ratio of count(S1 ∩ S2) and count(S1) needs not be the same as the ratio of count(S1 ∩ S2) and count(S2). The data association analysis is only performed for (S1 ∩ S2) when the ratio is greater than a specified threshold. Assume that (S1 ∩ S2) is shown in Figure 8-9.

Figure 8-9   Table of records for (S1 ∩ S2)

account#	name	age	sex
123	smith	22	M
456	susan	24	F
222	richard	27	M
777	ted	36	M

Using the membership functions in Figure 8-6 for "age," we obtain the following fuzzy symbol table:

Figure 8-10   The fuzzy symbol table for Figure 8-9

account#	name	age	sex
123	smith	young	M
456	susan	young	F
222	richard	young	M
777	ted	middle_age	M

The fuzzy sum-of-products for Figure 8-10 is

$$
\begin{aligned}
\text{association.high} \quad = \quad & (\text{age.young})(\text{sex.M}) + \\
& (\text{age.young})(\text{sex.F}) + \\
& (\text{age.young})(\text{sex.M}) + \\
& (\text{age.middle\_age})(\text{sex.M}) \\[6pt]
= \quad & (\text{age.young})(\text{sex.M}) + \\
& (\text{age.young})(\text{sex.F}) + \\
& (\text{age.middle\_age})(\text{sex.M}) \\[6pt]
= \quad & (\text{age.young})[\text{sex.M} + \text{sex.F}] \\
& (\text{age.middle\_age})(\text{sex.M}) \\[6pt]
= \quad & (\text{age.young}) + \\
& (\text{age.middle\_age})(\text{sex.M})
\end{aligned}
$$

Note that [sex.M + sex.F] is a tautology. Therefore, it is eliminated. Since the fuzzy sub-expression, (age.young), accounts for 75% of the cases in Figure 8-10, it may be used to *approximately* characterize the purchasing association of "beer" and "potato chips." This means that if a customer is young and if he/she buys beer, he/she is likely to buy potato chips as well.

References

Cook, D.J., Holder, L.B., and Djoko, S. [1996] "Scalable discovery of informative structural concepts using domain knowledge," *IEEE Expert*, October 1996, pp. 59-68.

Ezawa, K.J., and Norton, S.W. [1996] "Constructing Bayesian networks to predict uncollectible telecommunications accounts," *IEEE Expert*, October 1996, pp. 45-51.

Fayyad, U.M. [1996] "Data mining and knowledge discovery: Making sense out of data," *IEEE Expert*, October 1996, pp. 20-25.

Fogarty, K. [1994] "Data mining can help to extract jewels of data," *Network World*, June 6, 1994, pp. 40.

Gerber, C. [1996] "Excavate your data," *Datamation*, May 1, 1996, pp. 40-43.

Grupe, F.H., and Owrang, M.M. [1995] "Data mining: Issues and considerations," Department of Accounting and Computer Information Systems, University of Nevada, Reno, Nevada 89557-0016.

Grygo, E.M. [1995] "Data mining takes on a new look," *Client/Server Computing*, December 1995, pp. 23-24.

Hedberg, S.R. [1996] "Searching for the mother lode: tales of the first data miners," *IEEE Expert*, October 1996, pp. 4-7.

Hung, C.C., and Fernandez, B. [1993] "Minimizing rules of fuzzy logic system by using a systematic approach," *Proceedings of the 2nd IEEE International Conference on Fuzzy Systems*, IEEE Catalog Number 93CH3136-9, pp. 38-44, IEEE Service Center, 445 Hoes Lane, Box 1331, Piscataway, NJ 08855-1331, Tel. 800-678-4333, 908-981-0060, Fax 908-981-1721.

John, G.H., Miller, P., and Kerber, R. [1996] "Stock selection using rule induction," *IEEE Expert*, October 1996, pp. 52-58.

Lee, H.Y., and Ong, H.L. [1996] "Visualization support for data mining," *IEEE Expert*, October 1996, pp. 69-75.

Lewinson, L. [1993] "Data mining: Intelligent technology gets down to business," *PC AI*, November/December 1993, pp. 16-23.

Manji, J. [1996] "Data mining at Bayer strikes it mother lode," *Managing Automation*, pp. 64E-64H.

Mark, B. [1996] "Data mining — Here we go again?," *IEEE Expert*, October 1996, pp. 18-19.

Mesrobian, E., Muntz, R., Shek, E., Nittel, S., Rouche, M.L., Kriguer, M., Mechoso, C., Farrara, J., Stolorz, P., and Nakamura, H. [1996] " Mining geophysical data for knowledge," *IEEE Expert*, October 1996, pp. 34-44.

Moxon, B. [1996] "Defining data mining," *DBMS*, August 1996, pp. S11-S14.

Parsaye, K. [1995] "Large-scale data mining in parallel," Parallel Database Special, *DBMS*, March 1995, pp. H-J.

Rauen, C. [1995] "Mining for data," *Beyond Computing*, October 1995, pp. 23-26.

Simoudis, E. [1996] "Reality check for data mining," *IEEE Expert*, October 1996, pp. 26-33.

Slagle, J.R., Chang, C.L., and Lee, R.C.T. [1970] "A new algorithm for generating prime implicants," *IEEE Trans. on Computers*, Vol.C-19, No.4, April 1970, pp.304-310.

Weldon, J-L. [1996] "Data mining and visualization," *Database Programming & Design*, May 1996, pp. 21-24.

Chapter 9   Advanced Topics

Since the introduction of the NICEL language in [Nicesoft 1994], it has been used to represent algorithms for many real-world applications. In this chapter, it will be explained how the Sugeno-Takagi-Kang model can be represented in NICEL. Furthermore, extensions of NICEL will also be discussed.

In general, using common sense knowledge or the rule discovery techniques given in Chapter 8, it is usually not too difficult to decide fuzzy quantifications for variables and write fuzzy rules in a fuzzy program. The most tedious part is fine-tuning parameters of the membership functions of the fuzzy quantifications. In this chapter, some algorithms for adjusting parameters of membership functions in a fuzzy program will be given.

The Sugeno-Takagi-Kang Model

The Sugeno-Takagi-Kang model was proposed in [Takagi and Sugeno 1985, Sugeno and Kang 1988]. In this model, a fuzzy rule has the following form:

$$\text{if } x1 \text{ is } f1 \text{ and } ... \text{ and } xn \text{ is } fn \text{ then } y = co + c1*x1 + ... + cn*xn$$

where $x1,...,xn$ are input variables; $f1,...,fn$ are fuzzy quantifications; $c0,...,cn$ are constants; and y is an output variable defined by a linear function. Note that the singleton method is equivalent to a fuzzy rule where $y = c0$.

When evaluating this fuzzy rule, the fuzzification is the same as before. This means that the minimum of $f1(x1),...,fn(xn)$ is used as a weight for y. If there is more than one fuzzy rule for y, the weighted average is used. For example, consider the following three fuzzy rules:

> if $x1$ is F1 and $x2$ is G1 then $y = c0 + c1*x1 + c2*x2$
> if $x1$ is F2 then $y = d0 + d1*x1$
> if $x1$ is F3 and $x2$ is G2 then $y = e0 + e1*x1 + e2*x2$

The computation of the value of y is shown in Figure 9-1.

Figure 9-1   Computation of the value of the output variable y

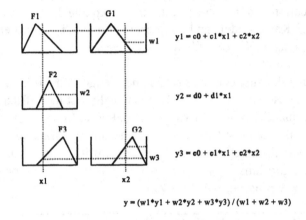

Figure 9-2   Data fitted by a piecewise linear function

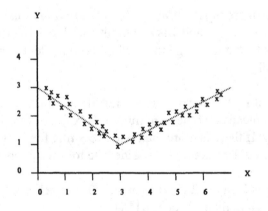

Intuitively, we can look at this kind of fuzzy rule as a way to specify a piecewise linear function. The left hand side of a fuzzy rule defines a fuzzy region where the linear function in the right hand side should be applied. In fact, if there is more than one fuzzy rule for the output variable y, all of the left hand sides of the fuzzy rules are evaluated to classify the input variables x1,...,xn. This determines which linear function will be used for computing y. If the pattern recognition interpretation discussed in Chapter 5 is used, the value of the output variable will be computed by using the linear function in the fuzzy rule whose left hand side is evaluated to be the largest. For example, consider the data shown in Figure 9-2.

Clearly, these data can be fitted by a piecewise linear function defined by the following two fuzzy rules:

if x is small then y = 3 - 0.667x;
if x is large then y = -0.5 + 0.5x;

As mentioned above, there are two ways to compute the value of y. One approach is to use the weighted average as proposed in [Takagi and Sugeno 1985, Sugeno and Kang 1988]. The other one is to use the pattern recognition method to choose a linear function for y. For example, if x=1, then since the value of the membership function for "small" is greater than the one for "large," the first linear function, namely, y=3 - 0.667x will be used. If x=5, then since the value of the membership function for "large" is greater than the one for "small," the second linear function, namely, y=-0.5 + 0.5x will be used.

As discussed in [Wang and Langari 1994], the difficulty of using the Sugeno-Takagi-Kang model is estimating coefficients in linear functions. The advantage of using the pattern recognition method for this model is that the coefficients can be estimated from training data by using the piecewise linear regression method [Draper and Smith 1966].

Fuzzy rules in the Sugeno-Takagi-Kang model can be represented in NICEL in two stages. For example, consider the two fuzzy rules for the data shown in Figure 9-2. First, the output variables linear1 and linear2 are introduced for the first and second fuzzy rules, respectively. Then, a fuzzy program as shown in Figure 9-3 is written.

Figure 9-3   A fuzzy program for the two fuzzy rules

```
* plinear.nl */

/* Copyright © 1996 by Nicesoft Corporation */

/*
x=input variable x;
linear1=output variable for the first fuzzy rule;
linear2=output variable for the second fuzzy rule;
*/

membership pack_1(v;a,b,c,d,e)
{
    define small by trapezoid(0,0,a,b);
    define large by trapezoid(c,d,e,e);
}

membership pack_2(v;a,b,c,d,e)
{
    define low by trapezoid(0,0,a,b);
    define high by trapezoid(c,d,e,e);
}

procedure plinear(x;
             linear1,linear2;
             a1,b1,c1,d1,e1,
             a2,b2,c2,d2,e2)
{
    use pack_1(x;a1,b1,c1,d1,e1);
    use pack_2(linear1,a2,b2,c2,d2,e2);
    use pack_2(linear2,a2,b2,c2,d2,e2);
```

if x is small then linear1 is high;

if x is large then linear2 is high;

}

_____

The above fuzzy program is compiled. Then, the procedure plinear can be called to compute values of linear1 and linear2 for a given value of x. If the weighted average method is used, y is computed as follows:

```
plinear(x,linear1,linear2,a1,b1,c1,d1,e1,a2,b2,c2,d2,e2);
y1 =  3 - 0.667*x;
y2 = -0.5 + 0.5*x;
y = (linear1*y1 + linear2*y2) / (linear1 + linear2);
```

If the pattern recognition method is used, y is computed as follows:

```
plinear(x,linear1,linear2,a1,b1,c1,d1,e1,a2,b2,c2,d2,e2);
if (linear1 >= linear2)
    y =  3 - 0.667*x;
else y = -0.5 + 0.5*x;
```

Extensions of The NICEL Language

In NICEL, a fuzzy rule has the form

if A1 is F1 and ... and An is Fn then B is G;

where A1,...,An, B are numerical variables and F1,...,Fn, G are fuzzy quantifications. Each "Ai is Fi" or "B is G" is called a fuzzy literal, where i=1,...,n. Each "Ai is Fi" represents a soft condition.

One way to extend NICEL is to allow the left hand side of a fuzzy rule to contain soft conditions as well as hard conditions. A hard condition is defined by using the following comparators: ==, <>, <, <=, >, and >=. If the left and right hand sides of a comparator are arithmetic expressions, they must be constructed from constants and numerical input variables and can be evaluated to numerical values. For example, the following fuzzy rule contains a hard condition defined by an inequality:

if x+y > 100 and x is large then z is small;

If s is a string input variable, the following hard condition can be used:

s == "constant string", or
s <> "constant string".

For example, consider the following fuzzy rule:

if sex == "male" and age is young then hair_length is short;

Here, we do not need to code "male" and "female" into numbers and define membership functions for them.

A hard condition will be evaluated to be 0 (false) or 1 (true). When performing fuzzification of a fuzzy rule, the minimum of the values computed from all of the hard and soft conditions in the left hand side of the fuzzy rule will be used as a weight for the output value.

Machine Training of Fuzzy Rules

Machine training is also called machine learning. The machine training problem is often treated as an optimization problem. The goal is to adjust a set of parameters in order to minimize an error function or to maximize performance criteria. The following is a list of applications or problems that can be tackled by machine training:

Function Approximation:

This is the same type of application as regression analysis or curve fitting. Assume that there is an unknown function,

$$y = f(x1,...,xn),$$

where x1,...,xn are input variables and y is an output variable. We first collect a set of data for the input and output variables. This set is called a *training set*. The output values in the training set are called observed values. For example, in the car-parallel parking or truck docking problem, a training set can be collected by having an expert driver performed the parallel parking or docking while automatically sampling the measurements from the sensors for the input and outout variables at every fixed time interval.

Next, a model is used to approximate the function. The model often contains a set of parameters. The goal is to adjust the parameters so that the sum of deviations (errors) between the observed and estimated output values is minimized.

In this book, a fuzzy program is used as a model to approximate a function. Fuzzy rules in the fuzzy program can be obtained by common sense knowledge or by using the techniques described in Chapter 8. The following is an example that illustrates how to adjust parameters of membership functions that define the fuzzy quantifications used in the fuzzy rules.

Consider the function, y=sin(x), as shown in Figure 9-4.

Figure 9-4   Function y=sin(x) for x from 0 to 3.1416

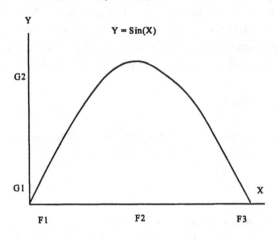

Assume that the following training set is used:

Index n	Variable x	Variable y
1	0.0000	0.0000
2	0.3927	0.3827
3	0.7854	0.7071
4	1.1781	0.9239
5	1.5708	1.0000
6	1.9635	0.9239
7	2.3562	0.7071
8	2.7489	0.3827
9	3.1416	0.0000

The fuzzy quantifications F1, F2, and F3 for variable x and G1 and G2 for variable y are defined by the membership functions shown in Figure 9-5.

Figure 9-5	Membership functions for F1, F2, F3, G1 and G2

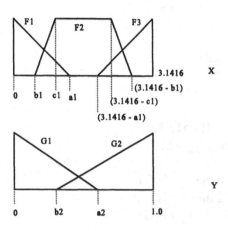

A fuzzy program that approximates the function in Figure 9-4 is given in Figure 9-6.

Figure 9-6	A fuzzy program approximating y = sin(x)

```
/* sine.nl */
/* Copyright © 1996 by Nicesoft Corporation */
/*
x=Value of the input variable x;
yy=Estimated value of output variable y;
*/

membership pack_1(v;a,b,c)
{
    define F1 by triangle(0,0,a);
    define F2 by trapezoid(b,c,3.1416-c,3.1416-b);
    define F3 by triangle(3.1416-a,3.1416,3.1416);
}
```

```
membership pack_2(v;a,b)
{
    define G1 by triangle(0,0,a);
    define G2 by triangle(b,1,1);
}

procedure sine(x; yy;
                a1,b1,c1,
                a2,b2)
{
    use pack_1(x;a1,b1,c1);
    use pack_2(yy;a2,b2);

    if x is F1 then yy is G1;
    if x is F2 then yy is G2;
    if x is F3 then yy is G1;
}
```

The above fuzzy program will be compiled, and given a set of
parameters a1, b1, c1, a2, and b2, for each value x(n) of the variable
x in the training set, the procedure

$$\text{sine}(x(n),yy(n),a1,b1,c1,a2,b2)$$

can be called to compute the value of yy(n), n=1,...,9. The error
between the observed value y(n) in the training set and the estimated
(approximate) value yy(n) is defined as

$$\text{error} = \Sigma \ (y(n) - yy(n))^{**}2 \qquad \text{over } n=1,...,9.$$

The problem is finding an optimal set of parameters a1, b1, c1, a2,
and b2 that minimize the error. From Figure 9-5, the parameters
need to satisfy the following set of constraints

$$0 <= a1 <= 3.1416,$$
$$0 <= b1 <= c1 <= 1.5708,$$
$$0 <= a2 <= 1,$$
$$0 <= b2 <= 1.$$

To solve the above optimization problem subject to the contraints, the gradient method can be used. The method begins with an initial set of parameters $a1(0)$, $b1(0)$, $c1(0)$, $a2(0)$, and $b2(0)$, and iteratively adjusts $a1(k)$, $b1(k)$, $c1(k)$, $a2(k)$, and $b2(k)$, $k=0,1,2,3, ...$, according to the following formulas:

$$a1(k+1) = a1(k) + \Delta a1(k),$$
$$b1(k+1) = b1(k) + \Delta b1(k),$$
$$c1(k+1) = c1(k) + \Delta c1(k),$$
$$a2(k+1) = a2(k) + \Delta a2(k),$$
$$b2(k+1) = b2(k) + \Delta b2(k),$$

Ordinarily, $\Delta a1(k)$, $\Delta b1(k)$, $\Delta c1(k)$, $\Delta a2(k)$ and $\Delta b2(k)$ will be set to a constant times the derivative of the error with respect to $a1$, $b1$, $c1$, $a2$ and $b2$. However, in this case, since the error involves the fuzzy program, the derivative is complicated. Therefore, the above formulas are not applicable. Instead, we will use the algorithm described as follows:

(1)   Start with an initial set of parameters $a1$, $b1$, $c1$, $a2$, and $b2$.

(2)   Adjust $a1$ by using the assignment
$$a1 \leftarrow a1 + \lambda 1$$
where $\lambda 1$ is the optimal real number that minimizes the error among the sets of parameters,
$$\{a1+\lambda, b1, c1, a2, b2\},$$
subject to the constraints.

(3)   Adjust $b1$ by using the assignment
$$b1 \leftarrow b1 + \lambda 2$$
where $\lambda 2$ is the optimal real number that minimizes the error among the sets of parameters,
$$\{a1, b1+\lambda, c1, a2, b2\},$$
subject to the constraints.

(4)   Adjust $c1$ by using the assignment
$$c1 \leftarrow c1 + \lambda 3$$
where $\lambda 3$ is the optimal real number that minimizes the error among the sets of parameters,
$$\{a1, b1, c1+\lambda, a2, b2\},$$

subject to the constraints.

(5)   Adjust a2 by using the assignment

$$a2 \leftarrow a2 + \lambda4$$

where $\lambda4$ is the optimal real number that minimizes the error among the sets of parameters,

$$\{a1, b1, c1, a2+\lambda, b2\},$$

subject to the constraints.

(6)   Adjust b2 by using the assignment

$$b2 \leftarrow b2 + \lambda5$$

where $\lambda5$ is the optimal real number that minimizes the error among the sets of parameters,

$$\{a1, b1, c1, a2, b2+\lambda\},$$

subject to the constraints.

(7)   Repeat (2) - (6) for a specified number of times, or until no further improvements are obtained.

In each of Steps (2) through (6), the optimal real number is obtained by testing each of λ set to

$$-m*\delta, -(m-1)*\delta, ..., -\delta, 0, \delta, 2*\delta, ..., (m-1)*\delta, m*\delta,$$

where m is a positive integer and δ is a small positive number.

Pictorially, the above algorithm is the same as sliding each of a1, b1, and c1 along the X-axis and sliding each of a2 and b2 along the Y-axis in Figure 9-5 while observing if the error is reduced. It is possible that the above algorithm may converge to a set of parameters a1, b1, c1, a2, and b2 where only the local minimum of the error is obtained. To get the global minimum of the error, the above algorithm can be run with many different initial sets of the parameters.

Pattern Recognition:

In a pattern recognition problem (e.g., speech recognition), data can be collected from different classes (e.g., phonemes). For example, consider the following data:

Pattern	Variable x1	Variable x2	Class
1	2.0	10	1
2	2.5	20	1
3	3.5	15	1
4	2.0	30	1
5	3.0	40	1
6	4.5	30	1
7	4.0	50	1
8	6.0	20	1
9	6.0	40	1
10	4.5	20	1
11	1.0	40	1
12	2.0	50	1
13	5.0	45	1
14	6.0	55	2
15	5.0	60	2
16	7.0	40	2
17	8.0	50	2
18	7.0	60	2
19	8.0	70	2
20	9.0	50	2
21	6.0	80	2
22	9.5	80	2
23	7.0	80	2
24	8.0	60	2
25	8.5	40	2
26	6.5	70	2

This set of data is called a *training set*. The data are shown in Figure 9-7, where class 1 and class 2 are denoted by "x" and "o," respecitively.

Figure 9-7   A training set for pattern recognition

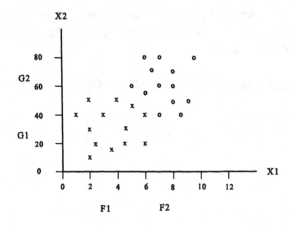

Figure 9-8   Membership functions for F1, F2, G1 and G2

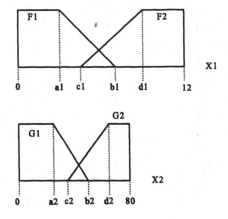

The fuzzy quantifications F1 and F2 for variable x1, and G1 and G2 for variable x2 are defined as shown in Figure 9-8. A fuzzy program for classifying the patterns in the training set is given in Figure 9-9.

Figure 9-9   A fuzzy program for pattern recognition

```
/* recog.nl */
/*
Copyright © 1996 by Nicesoft Corporation
*/

/*
x1=Variable x1;
x2=Variable x2;
class1=Class 1;
class2=Class 2;
*/

membership pack_1(v;a,b,c,d)
{
    define F1 by trapezoid(0,0,a,b);
    define F2 by trapezoid(c,d,12,12);
}

membership pack_2(v;a,b,c,d)
{
    define G1 by trapezoid(0,0,a,b);
    define G2 by trapezoid(c,d,12,12);
}

membership pack_3(v;a,b,c,d)
{
    define low by trapezoid(0,0,a,b);
    define high by trapezoid(c,d,12,12);
}
```

```
procedure recog(x1,x2; class1,class2;
                a1,b1,c1,d1,
                a2,b2,c2,d2,
                a3,b3,c3,d3,)
{
    use pack_1(x1;a1,b1,c1,d1);
    use pack_2(x2;a2,b2,c2,d2);
    use pack_3(class1;a3,b3,c3,d3);
    use pack_3(class2;a3,b3,c3,d3);

    if x1 is F1 and x2 is G1 then class1 is high;

    if x1 is F2 and x2 is G2 then class2 is high;
}
```

The above fuzzy program will be compiled, and given a set of
parameters a1, b1, c1, d1, a2, b2, c2, d2, a3, b3, c3, and d3, for each
pattern n in the training set, the procedure

$$recog(x1,x2,class1,class2,a1,b1,c1,d1,a2,b2,c2,d2,a3,b3,c3,d3)$$

can be called to compute the the values of class1 and class2, which
are then used to classify the pattern, n=1,...,26. The error is defined
as the number of patterns which are incorrectly classified.

The problem is finding an optimal set of parameters a1, b1, c1, d1,
a2, b2, c2, d2, a3, b3, c3, and d3 that minimizes the error, subject to
the following set of constraints obtained from Figure 9-8:

$$0 <= a1 <= b1 <= 12,$$
$$0 <= c1 <= d1 <= 12,$$
$$0 <= a2 <= b2 <= 80,$$
$$0 <= c2 <= d2 <= 80.$$

The same algorithm given for function approximation can be used.
That is, starting with an initial set of parameters a1, b1, c1, d1, a2,
b2, c2, d2, a3, b3, c3, and d3, we will first adjust a1, then b1, and so
on. Repeat this loop for a specified number of times, or until no

further improvements are achieved.

System Performance Optimization:

In the truck docking problem, data for the input variables (e.g., truck angle) and output variables (e.g., steering wheel angle) can be collected by sampling the measurements from the sensors that measure the input and output variables while an expert driver performs the docking of a truck. This set of collected data will be used as a training set. Using the methods discussed in Chapter 8 and this section, a fuzzy program based on the training set can be developed and written. Then, using the algorithm described above, the fuzzy program can be fine-tuned by adjusting the parameters of the membership functions one at a time. The end result is a fuzzy program that approximately mimics the expert driver. Now, the question is "how good is this fuzzy program?"

To answer this question, we need to specify system performance criteria. For the truck docking problem, the system performance criteria may be specified in terms of the truck path from the start to the end and the total time it takes to finish the docking. The goal is to minimize the total docking time and obtain a good final truck position, which is measured in terms of the distance between the truck and the middle of the dock, and the angle of the truck relative to the dock. This is clearly a multiple performance criterion problem. A fuzzy program can be used to define an overall system performance criterion in terms of the component system performance criteria. Once the overall system performance criterion is defined, we then give a test run of the fuzzy system with a set of parameters of the membership functions, and collect data to compute the overall system performance criterion. The test run of the fuzzy system can be repeated with a new set of parameters which are obtained by using the algorithm described for function approximation. Hopefully, a set of parameters can be found that results in a better system performance than the expert driver's performance.

As described above, most control systems have more than one

system performance criterion. For example, when designing a setpoint control system, the goal is to achieve the minimum time to reach to the setpoint with the minimum overshooting. Similarly, in developing a sprinkler control system, the objective is to accomplish the minimum consumption of water and the maximum yield of the crop. These criteria are often contradictory. Therefore, we need to find a way to combine them into an overall system performance criterion. As it turns out, a fuzzy program can be written to define the overall system performance. For example, Figure 9-10 shows such a fuzzy program for the truck docking problem.

Figure 9-10   A fuzzy program for defining an overall performance

```
/* perform.nl */
/*
Copyright © 1996 by Nicesoft Corporation
*/

/*
tim=Toatl docking time;
dis=Distance between the truck and the middle of the dock;
ang=abs(TruckAngle - 90);
perf=Overall system performance;
*/

membership pack_1(x;a,b,c,d,e,f,g,h,h)
{
    define low by trapezoid(0,0,a,b);
    define medium by triangle(c,d,e);
    define high by trapezoid(f,g,h,h);
}

procedure perform(tim,dis,ang; perf;
                a1,b1,c1,d1,e1,f1,g1,h1,
                a2,b2,c2,d2,e2,f2,g2,h2,
                a3,b3,c3,d3,e3,f3,g3,h3,
                a4,b4,c4,d4,e4,f4,g4,h4)
```

```
{
    use pack_1(tim;a1,b1,c1,d1,e1,f1,g1,h1);
    use pack_1(dis;a2,b2,c2,d2,e2,f2,g2,h2);
    use pack_1(ang;a3,b3,c3,d3,e3,f3,g3,h3);
    use pack_1(perf;a4,b4,c4,d4,e4,f4,g4,h4);

    if tim is small and dis is small and ang is small
            then perf is high;
    if tim is medium and dis is small and ang is small
            then perf is high;
    if time is large and dis is small and ang is small
            then perf is medium;
    if ang is large then perf is low;
    if ang is medium the perf is low;
    if dis is large then perf is low;
    if dis is medium then perf is low;

}
```

References

Draper, N.R., and Smith, H. [1966] *Applied Regression Analysis*, John Wiley & Sons, New York, 1966.

Hung, C.C. [1993] "Building a neuro-fuzzy learning control system," *AI Expert*, November 1993, pp. 40-49.

Nicesoft [1994] *Decision Plus User's Handbook*, Nicesoft Corporation, 9215 Ashton Ridge, Austin, TX 78750, USA, Phone (512) 331-9027, Fax (512) 219-5837.

Sugeno, M., and Kang, G.T. [1988] "Structure identification of fuzzy model," *Fuzzy Sets Systems*, Vol. 28, 1988, pp. 15-33.

Takagi, T., and Sugeno, M. [1985] "Fuzzy identification of systems and its applications to modeling and control," *IEEE Transaction on Systems, Man and Cybernectics*, Vol. 15, 1985, pp. 116-132.

Wang, L., and Langari, R. [1994] Building Sugeno-type models using fuzzy discretization and orthogonal parameter estimation techniques," *Proceedings of the 1994 North American Fuzzy Information Processing Society Conference*, IEEE Catalog Number 94TH8006, pp. 132-135, IEEE Service Center, 445 Hoes Lane, Box 1331, Piscataway, NJ 08855-1331, Tel. 800-678-4333, 908-981-0060, Fax 908-981-1721.

Appendix A.   Tranducers and Sensors Vendors

Adsens Tech Inc, 18310 Bedford Circle, La Puente, Ca 91744 USA,
Phone 818-854-2772, Fax 818-854-2776. *This company
provides laser analog displacement sensors.*

AM Sensors Inc, 26 Keewaydin Drive, Salem, NH 03079-2839,
USA, Phone 800-289-2611, 603-898-1543,
Fax 603-898-1638. *This company manufactures non-contact
microwave proximity, direction, displacement, level, and
velocity sensors.*

Aromat Corporation, Factory Automation, 629 Central Avenue,
New Providence, NJ 07974, USA, Phone 1-800-228-2350,
Fax 908-464-8513. *This company provides laser sensors,
and photoelectric sensors and switches.*

Advanced Thermal Products, P.O. Box 249, 328 Ridgway Road,
St. Marys, PA 15857, Phone 814-834-1541,
Fax 814-834-1556. *This company provides temperature
sensing probes and assemblies.*

Banner Engineering Corporation, 9714 10th Ave North,
Minneapolis, MN 55441, USA, Phone 612-544-3164,
Fax 612-544-3213. *This company manufactures over
10,000 different photoelectric sensors for detecting objects
through light reflection. Detecting ranges can be from a few
inches to 65 feet.*

BEI Sensors & Systems Company [1995] "Sensor Integration,"
Tustin, Ca, Phone 714-258-7500. *This project takes
company's existing sensor devices, such as contact position
sensors used for a number of applications in the
transportation industry, and adds more active circuitry.*

Control Engineering [1996] "What the devil is that level?" *Control Engineering*, June 1996, pp.51-56. *This article reports many direct level sensing products used in chemical/petrochemical, petroleum, and water/wastewater applications.*

Data Instruments Inc, 100 Discovery Way, Acton, MA 01720-3600, USA, Phone 508-264-9550, Fax 508-263-0630. *This company manufactures pressure sensors, pressure transmitters, load cells, and linear displacement transducers.*

Druck Inc, 4 Dunham Drive, New Fairfield, CT 06812, USA, Phone 203-746-0400, Fax 203-746-2494. *This company manufactures pressure transducers and pressure transmitters.*

Efector Inc, 805 Springdale Drive, Exton, PA 19341,USA, Phone 215-524-2000, Fax 215-524-2010. *This company manufactures inductive and capacitive proximity switches and sensors. Detection ranges are from 0.8 to 120 mm. Examples of applications are liquid level sensing, grain, plastic pellets or other granular/powdered material sensing, belt/wire breakage detecting, the end of the roll detecting, sealed material measuring, etc.*

Electronic Products [1995] "Pressure and temperature sensors," *Electronic Products*, pp.57-67, May 1995. *This magazine lists and describes some pressure and temperature products.*

Electronic Products [1996] "Update on pressure and temperature sensors," *Electronic Products*, pp.33-38, February 1996. *This magazine lists pressure and temperature sensors.*

Entran Devices Inc, 10 Washington Avenue, Fairfield, NJ 07004, USA, Phone 201-227-1002, Fax 201-227-6865. *This company manufactures pressure transducers, load cells, strain gauges,accelerometers, and pressure transmitters.*

Fargo Controls Inc, P.O. Box 539, 20 Hampton Road, Eatontown,
NJ 07724, USA, Phone 908-389-3376, Fax 908-542-3553.
*This company provides inductive, capacitive, ultrasonic,
photo-electric, and magnetic proximity sensors.*

Fenwal Electronics Inc, 450 Fortune Boulevard, Milford, MA
01757-1745, USA, Phone 508-478-6000, Fax 508-473-6035.
This company provides disc thermistors.

Ferran Scientific, 11558 Sorrento Valley Road, San Diego,
CA 92121, USA, Phone 619-792-2332, Fax 619-793-0065.
*This company provides micropole sensors for gas analysis,
mass spectrum analysis, process monitoring, and leak
detection.*

Gordon Products Inc, 67 Del Mar Drive, Brookfield, CT,
06804-2494, USA, Phone 203-775-4501, Fax 203-775-1162.
*This company provides analog proximity sensors, eddy
current proximity switches, standard sensitivity loop sensors,
high sensitivity ring sensors, capacitive proximity switches,
and inductive proximity switches.*

Hayashi Denkoh Co. Ltd., 5-5, 6-Chome, Honkomagome,
Bunkyo-Ku, Tokyo 113, Japan, Phone 03-3945-3151,
Fax 03-3945-3130. *This company provides platinum
thin-film temperature detectors.*

Idec Corporation, 1213 Elko Drive, Sunnyvale, CA 94089,
USA, Phone 408-747-0550, Fax 408-744-9055.
*This company provides color sensors, ultrasonic
distance sensors, laser displacement sensors, and
photoelectric sensors.*

LEM U.S.A. Inc, 6643 West Mill Road, Milwaukee,
WI 53218, USA, Phone 414-353-0711,
Fax 414-353-0733. *This company manufactures current
and voltage transducers.*

Lucas NovaSensor, 1055 Mission Court, Fremont, CA 94539, USA, Phone 510-490-9100, Fax 510-770-0645. *This company provides solid state pressure sensors and silicon accelerometers.*

Magnetek, 650 Easy Street, Simi Valley, CA 93065, USA, Phone 805-581-3985, Fax 805-583-1526. *This company manufactures a wide range of pressure transducers, position/velocity sensors, accelerometers, and load cells.*

Motorola Sensor Products Division, Motorola Literature Distribution, P.O.Box 20912, Phoenix, Arizona 85036, USA, MFAX: RMFAX0@email.sps.mot.com - (602) 244-6609, INTERNET: http://Design-NET.com. *This division provides pressure, acceleration, chemical, and biomedical sensors.*

Murata Erie North America, 2200 Lake Park Drive, Smyrna, Georgia 30080, USA, Phone 1-800-831-9172, Fax 404-684-1541. *This company provides infrared sensors, magnetic angle sensors, magnetoresistive sensors, rotational angle sensors, temperature sensors, airflow sensors, and thermistors.*

Novotechnik U. S.Inc, 237 Cedar Hill Street, Marlborough, MA 01752, Phone 508-485-2244, Fax 508-485-2430. *This company provides conductive-plastic position sensors, conductive-plastic rectilinear position transducers, and rotary conductive-plastic potentiometers.*

Omega Engineering Inc [1996] **The Data Acquisition Systems Handbook**, P.O. Box 4047, Satmford, CT 06907 USA Phone 1-800-826-6342, Fax 203-359-7700.

This handbook offers over 650 full-color pages
with products including communication-based systems
and plug-in cards for personal computers.

Omega Engineering Inc [1996] **The Electric Heaters
Handbook,** P.O. Box 4047, Satmford, CT 06907 USA
Phone 1-800-826-6342, Fax 203-359-7700.
This handbook offers equipment for thousands of industrial
and lab, electric heating and temperature control
applications. Over 700 color pages present heating cables,
strip, carridge, tubular, immersion, lab, specialty, and band
heaters.

Omega Engineering Inc [1996] **The Flow and Level
Handbook,** P.O. Box 4047, Satmford, CT 06907 USA
Phone 1-800-826-6342, Fax 203-359-7700.
This handbook has over 700 full-color pages
featuring a comprehensive selection of flow and level
measurement products and systems.

Omega Engineering Inc [1996] **The Green Book,** P.O. Box
4047, Satmford, CT 06907 USA,
Phone 1-800-826-6342, Fax 203-359-7700.
This book contains hundreds of devices for lab and
industrial monitoring and control of various
environment parameters. It includes water/wastewater
sampling, air flow and sampling, gas monitors and
alarms, test kits, leak detectors, pH and conductivity
devices, and more.

Omega Engineering Inc [1996] **The Infrared Temperature
Handbook,** P.O. Box 4047, Satmford, CT 06907 USA
Phone 1-800-826-6342, Fax 203-359-7700.
This handbook lists many infrared thermocouples for
non-contact surface measurements of temperature.

Omega Engineering Inc [1996] **The pH and Conductivity Handbook**, P.O. Box 4047, Satmford, CT 06907 USA Phone 1-800-826-6342, Fax 203-359-7700. *This handbook has over 500 full-color pages featuring electrodes and accessories, lab intrumentation, field service products, industrial control systems, auxiliary equipment, and data acquisition systems.*

Omega Engineering Inc [1996] **The Pressure, Strain and Force Handbook**, P.O. Box 4047, Satmford, CT 06907 USA Phone 1-800-826-6342, Fax 203-359-7700. *This handbook has over 700 full-color pages featuring pressure switches, load cells, strain guages, controllers, recorders, dataloggers, tranducers, and much more.*

Omega Engineering Inc [1996] **The Temperature Handbook**, P.O. Box 4047, Satmford, CT 06907 USA Phone 1-800-826-6342, Fax 203-359-7700. *This handbook has over 1500 full-color pages featuring a wide selection of temperature measurement and control products. It includes thermocouple probes and assemblies, handheld instruments, intelligent panel meters, recorders, wire, infrareds and more.*

R & D Magazine [1996] "Advanced fabrication technology leads to new senor possibilities," R & D Magazine, July 1996, pp. 23-26. *This article describes the technology for making medical sensors.*

Ramco Electronic Co, 1207 Maple Street, P.O. Box 65310, West Des Moines, IA 50265, USA, Phone 515-225-6933, Fax 515-225-0063. *This company provides laser beam sensors.*

RdF Corporation, 23 Elm Avenue, P.O. Box 490, Hudson, NH 03051, USA, Phone 800-445-8367, 603-882-5195, Fax 603-882-6925. *This company specializes in temperature measurement.*

Sensors Magazine, Helmers Publishing Inc, 174 Concord St., P.O. Box 874, Peterborough, NH 03458-0874, USA, Phone 603-924-9631, Fax 603-924-7408. *This magazine publishes SENSORS monthly, and is the sponsor of the annual Sensors Expo and Sensors Expo West Conferences and Expositions.*

Sensotec Inc, 1200 Chesapeake Avenue, Columbus, Ohio 43212-2288 USA, Phone 614-486-7723, 1-800-848-6564, Fax 614-486-0506. This company has transducers for pressure, force, and acceleration measurements.

Star Micronics, OEM Division, 70-D Ethel Road West, Piscataway, NJ 08854, USA, Phone 1-800-782-7636, 908-572-9512, Fax 908-572-5095. *This company manufactures miniature sound transducers and sound buzzers.*

Texmate, 995 Park Center Drive, Vista, CA 92083-8397, USA, Phone 1-800-394-8344, 619-598-9899, Fax 619-598-9828. *This company manufactures titanium pressure sensors which can be used with a variety of gases and liquids.*

Therm-O-Disc Inc, Subsidiary of Emerson Electric, 1320 South Main Street, Mansfield, Ohio 44907-0538, USA, Phone 419-525-8500, Fax 419-525-8344. *This company provides thermisters.*

Travis, B. [1996] "Smart sensors," _EDN_, pp.57-65, May 9,
    1996.

Tri-Tronics Company Inc, P.O. Box 25135, Tampa, Florida
    33622-5135, USA, Phone 813-886-4000,
    Fax 813-884-8818. _This company manufactures_
    photoelectric sensors.

Turck USA, 3000 Campus Drive, Minneapolis, MN
    55441, USA, Phone 612-553-7300, Fax 612-553-0708.
    This company provides a comprehensive selection of
    inductive, inductive magnet operated, capacitive, and
    ultrasonic proximity sensors.

Appendix B.   Data Acquisition Boards Vendors

Acces I/O Products Inc, 9400 Activity Road, San Diego, CA 92126
USA, Phone 619-693-9005, 800-326-1649,
Fax 619-578-9711. *This company supplies data acquisition
boards compatible with LABTECH NOTEBOOK from
Laboratory Technologies Corporation (P.O. Box 838,
Brockton, MA 02403 USA, Phone 800-899-1612,
Fax 800-899-1609).*

Advantech, 750 East Arques Avenue, Sunnyvale, CA 94086
USA, Phone 408-245-6678, Fax 408-245-8268. *This
company supplies data acquisition boards compatible with
LABTECH NOTEBOOK.*

American Data Acquisition Corporation, 70 Tower Office park,
Woburn, Massachusetts 01801, USA, Phone 617-935-3200,
Fax 617-938-6553. *This company supplies data acquisition
boards which work with DriverLINK, Snap-Master,
LABTECH NOTEBOOK, LabVIEW, and LabWindows/CVI.*

ComputerBoards Inc, 125 High Street, Mansfield, MA 02048 USA,
Phone 508-261-1123, Fax 508-261-1094. *This company
supplies data acquisition boards, and UniversalLibrary
Programmer's Interface for Windows and DOS languages
such as Microsoft Visual C++ & C, Visual Basic, Borland
C/C++, Watcom C and Pascal. The functions in the
UniversalLibrary is listed in Appendix D. It aslo provides
UniversalTools for Programmers which has a set of functions
as listed in Appendix E for data analysis and manipulation,
creating graphical objects for displaying data and user input,
and real time control. The company wants to help the user
get low prices for hardware with every brand of software
such as LabVIEW, LABTECH NOTEBOOK, Snap-Master,
DASYLab, or Real-Time Graphics Tools.*

CyberResearch Inc, 25 Business Park Drive, Branford,
    CT 06405, USA, Phone 203-483-8815, 800-341-2525,
    Fax 203-483-9024. *This company supplies data
    acquisition boards, and GPIB interface cards. It also
    offers software products such as icon-and-flow-chart-
    based LABTECH NOTEBOOKpro and SanpMaster, and
    VisualLab control extensions for use with Microsoft's
    Visual Basic and Visual C++.*

Data Translation, 100 Locke Drive, Marlboro, MA 01752-1192,
    USA, Phone 508-481-3700, 800-525-8528,
    Fax 508-481-8620. *This company provides data acquisition
    boards and image grabbers. It also offers LABTECH
    NOTEBOOKpro licensed from Laboratory Technologies
    Corporation. Its VB-EZ for Visual Basic provides a set of
    programming tools for developing data acquisition
    applications in Visual Basic.*

Intelligent Instrumentation, 1141 West Grant Road, MS131, Tucson,
    Arizona 85705 USA, Phone 602-623-9801,
    Fax 602-623-8965. *This company supplies data acquisition
    boards compatible with LABTECH NOTEBOOK.*

Keithley Metrabyte, 440 Myles Standish Boulevard, Taunton,
    MA 02780, USA, Phone 508-880-3000, 800-348-0033,
    Fax 508-880-0179. *This company supplies data
    acquisition boards and signal conditioning products.
    It also offers software products such as Visual Test
    Extensions (VTX), Windows drivers and DriverLINX
    for use with C/C++, Visual Basic, Delphi, or Pascal.*

National Instruments, 6504 Bridge Point Parkway, Austin, TX
    78730-5039 USA, Phone 512-794-0100, 800-433-3488,
    Fax 512-794-8411. *This company is one of the leading
    manufacturers that supplies data acquisition boards,
    GPIB interface products, VXI bus products, and signal
    conditioning products. National Instruments is well known
    for its software products such as LabVIEW and*

LabWindows/CVI. It also provides Driver DLL CD-ROM and ComponentWorks for Visual Basic and Visual C++ users.

National Instruments [1996] "INSTRUPEDIA 96," 6504 Bridge
    Point Parkway, Austin, TX 78730-5039 USA,
    Phone 512-794-0100, 800-433-3488, Fax 512-794-8411.

Omega Engineering Inc, P.O. Box 4047, Satmford, CT 06907 USA
    Phone 1-800-826-6342, Fax 203-359-7700.
    This company supplies data acquisition boards compatible with LABTECH NOTEBOOK.

Appendix C.   Functions in LabWindows/CVI

The list of DAQ functions in LabWindows:

A2000_Calibrate	A2000_Config	A2150_Calibrate
AI_Check	AI_Clear	AI_Configure
AI_Mux_Config AI_Read	AI_Read_Scan	AI_Setup
AI_VRead	AI_VRead_Scan	AI_VScale
Align_DMA_Buffer	AO_Calibrate	AO_Change_Parameter
AO_Configure	AO_Update	AO_VScale
AO_VWrite	AO_Write	Calibrate_1200
Calibrate_E_Series	Config_Alarm_Deadband	
Config_ATrig_Event_Message		
Config_DAQ_Event_Message		
Configure_HW_Analog_Trigger		
CTR_Config	CTR_ECount	CTR_EvRead
CTR_FOUT_Config	CTR_Period	CTR_Pulse
CTR_Rate	CTR_Reset	CTR_Restart
CTR_Simul_Op	CTR_Square	CTR_State
STR_Stop	DAQ_Check	DAQ_Clear
DAQ_Config	DAQ_DB_Config	DAQ_DB_HalfReady
DAQ_DB_StrTransfer	DAQ_DB_Transfer	DAQ_Monitor
DAQ_Op	DAQ_Rate	DAQ_Start
DAQ_StopTrigger_Config	DAQ_to_Disk	DAQ_VScale
DIG_Block_Check	DIG_Block_Clear	DIG_Block_In
DIG_Block_Out	DIG_Block_PG_Config	DIG_DB_Config
DIG_DB_HalfReady	DIG_DB_StrTransfer	DIG_DB_Transfer
DIG_Grp_Config	DIG_Grp_Mode	DIG_Grp_Status
DIG_In_Grp	DIG_In_Line	DIG_In_Port
DIG_Line_Config	DIG_Out_Grp	DIG_Out_Line
DIG_Out_Port	DIG_Prt_Config	DIG_Prt_Status
DIG_SCAN_Setup	DSP2200_Calibrate	DSP2200_Config
Get_DAQ_Device_Info	Get_DAQ_Event	Get_NI_DAQ_Version
GPCTR_Change_Parameter	GPCTR_Config_Buffer	GPCTR_Control
GPCTR_Set_Application	GPCTR_Watch	ICTR_Read
ICTR_Reset	ICTR_Setup	Init_DA_Brds
Lab_ISCAN_Check	Lab_ISCAN_Op	Lab_ISCAN_Start
Lab_ISCAN_to_Disk	LPM16_Calibrate	MAI_Arm
MAI_Clear	MAI_Coupling	MAI_Read
MAI_Scale	MAI_Setup	Master_Slave_Config
MDAQ_Check	MDAQ_Clear	MDAQ_Get
MDAQ_ScanRate	MDAQ_Setup	MDAQ_Start
MDAQ_Stop	MDAQ_StrGet	MDAQ_Trig_Delay
MDAQ_Trig_Select	MIO_Calibrate	MIO_Config
NI_DAQ_Mem_Alloc	NI_DAQ_Mem_Attributes	

NI_DAQ_Mem_Copy	NI_DAQ_Mem_Free	NI_DAQ_Mem_Lock
NI_DAQ_Mem_Unlock	Peek_DAQ_Event	REG_Level_Read
REG_Level_Write	RTSI_Clear	RTSI_Clock
RTSI_Conn	RTSI_DisConn	SC_2040_Config
SCAN_Demux	SCAN_Op	
SCAN_Sequence_Demux	SCAN_Sequence_Retrieve	
SCAN_Sequence_Setup	SCAN_Setup	SCAN_Start
SCAN_to_Disk	SCXI_AO_Write	SCXI_Cal_Constants
SCXI_Calibrate_Setup	SCXI_Change_Chan	SCXI_Configure_Filter
SCXI_Get_Chassis_Info	SCXI_Get_Module_Info	SCXI_Get_State
SCXI_Get_Status	SCXI_Load_Config	SCXI_MuxCtr_Setup
SCXI_Reset	SCXI_Scale	SCXI_SCAN_Setup
SCXI_Set_Config	SCXI_Set_Gain	SCXI_Set_Input_Mode
SCXI_Set_State	SCXI_Single_Chan_Setup	
SCXI_Track_Hold_Control	SCXI_Track_Hold_Setup	
Select_Signal	Set_DAQ_Device_Info	Timeout_Config
Trigger_Window_Config	USE_A2XXX	USE_AO_2DC
USE_AO_610	USE_DIO_24	USE_DIO_32F
USE_DIO_96	USE_DSP2200	USE_LAB
USE_LPM	USE_MIO	USE_TIO_10
USE_E_Series	USE_E_Series_AI	USE_E_Series_AO
USE_E_Series_DAQ	USE_E_Series_DIO	USE_E_Series_GPCTR
USE_E_Series_GPCTR_Simple		USE_E_Series_Misc
USE_E_Series_WFM	WFM_Chan_Control	WFM_Check
WFM_ClockRate	WFM_DB_Config	WFM_DB_HalfReady
WFM_DB_StrTransfer	WFM_DB_Transfer	WFM_from_Disk
WFM_Group_Control	WFM_Group_Setup	WFM_Load
WFM_Op	WFM_Rate	WFM_Scale

A sublist of GUI functions in LabWindows:

Control Functions:

DefaultCtrl	DiscardCtrl	DuplicateCtrl
GetActiveCtrl	GetCtrlAttribute	GetCtrlBoundingRect
GetCtrlVal	NewCtrl	SetActiveCtrl
SetCtrlAttribute	SetCtrlVal	

Control Functions for Text Boxes:

DeleteTextBoxLine	GetNewTextBoxLines	GetTextBoxLine
GetTextBoxLineLength	InsertTextBoxLine	ReplaceTextBoxLine
ResetTextBox		

Graph and Strip Chart Functions:

ClearStripChart	DeleteGraphPlot	GetActiveGraphCursor
GetAxisRange	GetCursorAttribute	GetGraphCursor
GetGraphCursorIndex	GetPlotAttribute	GetTraceAttribute
PlotArc	PlotBitmap	PlotIntensity
PlotLine	PlotOval	PlotPoint
PlotPolygon	PlotRectangle	PlotStripChart
PlotStripChartPoint	PlotText	PlotWaveform
PlotX	PlotXY	PlotY
SetActiveGraphCursor	SetAxisrange	SetCursorAttribute
SetGraphCursor	SetGraphCursorIndex	SetPlotAttribute
SetTraceAttribute		

ListBox and Ring Functions:

ClearListCtrl	DeleteListItem	GetCtrlIndex
GetIndexFromValue	GetLabelFromIndex	
GetLabelLengthFromIndex	GetNumListItems	GetValueFromIndex
GetValueLengthFromIndex	InsertListItem	ReplaceListItem
SetCtrlIndex		

MenuBar Functions:

DiscardMenu	DiscardMenuBar	DiscardMenuItem
DiscardSubMenu	EmptyMenu	EmptyMenuBar
GetMenuBarAttribute	GetPanelMenuBar	
GetSharedMenuBarEventPanel		InsertSeparator
LoadMenuBar	NewMenu	NewMenuBar
NewMenuItem	NewSubMenu	SetMenuBarAttribute
SetpanelMenuBar		

Panel Functions:

DefaultPanel	DiscardPanel	DisplayPanel
DuplicatePanel	GetActivePanel	GetPanelAttribute
HidePanel	LoadPanel	NewPanel
RecallPanelState	SavepanelState	SetActivePanel
SetPanelAttribute	SetPanelPos	

Pop-up Panel Functions:

ConfirmPopup	DirSelectPopup	FileSelectPopup
FontSelectPopup	GenericMessagePopup	
GetSystemPopupAttributes	InstallPopup	MessagePopup
MultifileSelectPopup	PromptPopup	RemovePopup
SetFontPopupDefaults	SetSystemPopupAttributes	
WaveformGraphPopup	XGraphPopup	XYGraphPopup
YGraphPopup		

Appendix D.   Functions in UniversalLibrary

ANALOG I/O:

cbAin	/* Single analog input */
cbAinScan	/* Input from ChLo to ChHi N times at R rate */
cbALoadQueue	/* Load channel/gain queue */
cbAout	/* Single analog output */
cbAoutScan	/* Output from ChLo to ChHi N times at R rate */
cbAPreTrig	/* Set pretrigger buffer and scan values */
cbATrig	/* Analog trigger setup */
cbAFileAinScan	/* Analog input direct to file */
cbFilePreTrig	/* Pre-triggered analog input to a file */
cbAConvertData	/* Converts analog input to channel/data format */
cbAConvertPretrigData	/* Unload & convert pretrigger data */
cbGetStatus	/* Return status of a background operation */
cbStopBackground	/* Halt a background process */

THERMOCOUPLE INPUT:

cbTIn	/* Inputs, smooths, compensates & linearizes TC */
cbTInScan	/* Same for a range of thermocouples */

COUNTER:

cbC8254Config	/* Select counter operating mode for 82C54 chip */
cb8536Config	/* Select operating mode for Z8536 chips */
cb8536Init	/* Set options for Z8536 chips */
cbC9513Config	/* Select operating mode for 9513 chips */
cbC9513Init	/* Set options for 9513 chips */
cbCFreqIn	/* Measure frequency using counters */
cbCIn	/* Read counter */
cbCLoad	/* Load counter value */
cbCStoreOnInt	/* Store counter value on interrupt */

DIGITAL I/O:

cbDBitIn	/* Input a single digital bit */
cbDBitOut	/* Output a single digital bit */
cbDConfigPort	/* Configure one port for input or output */
cbDIn	/* Input a single 8 bit port */
cbDInScan	/* Reads N bytes at R rate from one port */
cbDOut	/* Output a single 8 bit port */
cbDoutScan	/* Outputs N bytes at R rate to one port */

MEGA-FIFO MEMORY INPUT/OUTPUT FUNTIONS:
```
cbMemSetDTMode          /* Set direction of DT-connect transfer */
cbMemReset              /* Reset M-FIFO memory to start address */
cbMemRead               /* Read data from M-FIFO to data array */
cbMemWrite              /* Write from data array to M-FIFO memory */
cbMemReadPretrig        /* Read & organize pre-trigger data from M-F */
```

STREAMER FILE FUNCTIONS:
```
cbFileAinScan           /* ransfer analog input directly to streamer file */
cbFilePreTrig           /* Use pretrigger strategy to streamer file */
cbFileGetInfo           /* Reads acquisition parameters from file */
cbFileRead              /* Reads N data points into array from file */
```

ERROR HANDLING FUNCTIONS:
```
cbErrHandling           /* Selects from several types of error handling */
cbGetErrMsg             /* Converts error codes into English messages */
```

Appendix E.   Functions in UniversalTools

Function	Description
cbCalculation	Calculation function.
cbCalibration	Calibration function.
cbChangeAlarm	Change alarm handler setpoint.
cbCheckAlarm	Check data for any alarm using a specified handler.
cbCreateAnalogMeter	Create and display an analog meter.
cbCreateAnnunciator	Create and display an annunciator.
cbCreateBarMeter	Create and display a bar meter.
cbCreateDiff	Create a differentiator.
cbCreateDigitalMeter	Create and display a digital meter.
cbCreateKnob	Create and display a circular knob.
cbCreateLED	Create and display an LED.
cbCreateMAFilter	Create a moving average filter.
cbCreateMFilter	Create a median filter.
cbCreateScope	Create and display a digital oscilloscope.
cbCreateSGFilter	Create a Savitzky-Golay filter.
cbCreateSlider	Create and display a slider.
cbCreateStripChart	Create and display a scrolling strip chart.
cbCreateToggle	Create and display a toggle switch.
cbDestroyFilter	Destroy a filter when it is no longer needed.
cbDiff	Differentiate data in real time.
cbFreeAlarm	Destroy an alarm handler.
cbGetAlarm	Get the parameters for an alarm handler.
cbGetControlStruc	Get the properties of a specified GUI control.
cbGetStripChartMode	Get the mode (live or historical) of a strip chart.
cbGetValue	Get the value of an input GUI control.
cbMAFilter	Smooth data using a specified MA filter.
cbMFilter	Smooth data using a specified median filter.
cbRealFFT	Compute the FFT of real data.
cbRealFFTMag	Compute the magnitude of a specified harmonic.
cbSetControlStruc	Modify the properties of a specified GUI control.
cbSetStripChartMode	Set the mode (live or historical) of a strip chart.
cbSetupAlarm	Create an alarm handler with specified setpoints.
cbSGFilter	Smooth data using a specified SG filter.
cbStatistics	Compute statistics of a given data set.
cbThreeDFrame	Display a three dimensional frame.
cbUpdateBlock	Display a block of data on an oscilloscope.
cbUpdateDisplay	Display data on a specified GUI control.
cbUpdateLED	Change the status of an LED.
cbUpdateToggle	Change the status of a toggle switch.
cbXSIntegrate	Integrate a block of data with Simpson's rule.
cbXTIntegrate	Integrate a block of data with trapezoidal rule.

Apppendix F   Some Applications In Control

Automatic Transmission Control

Mitsubishi and Honda [Jurgen 1995] add fuzzy control to a conventional technique by wrapping up the driver's intentions, vehicle status, and road conditions into a final judgment. Based on that judgment, the system can select from a so-called flat mode (even terrain), one that climbs a curvy hill, one that climbs a straight hill, or one that goes downhill. A map for each mode decides on throttle opening and gear position according to vehicle speed, as is done with the usual type of automatic transmission.

Battery-Charger Control

National Semiconductor [Electronic Design 1995] has used neural netword/fuzzy-logic to develop an intelligent super-fast battery charger for batteries that meets cost, lifetime and speed requirements. This battery charger cut the traditional charge time from 1-1/2 hours to a mere 20 to 30 minutes while saving approximately 30% of the battery's life by avoiding overcharging, exceeding temperature limits, and exceeding safe-current charge limits.

Computer-Aided Train Dispatch

The project reported in [Vieira and Gomide 1996] develops a system that schedules trains to carry as much iron ore as set by a quota from a mine to a harbor while reducing the operating costs and ensuring safety. Information used by the system include train data such as position, speed, direction, number of cars, priority, fuel level, number of locomotives, and repair conditions of each train; track information such as steepness, switch status, single or double track; operators' shifts; and the status of loading and unloading equipment at the mine and the harbor. Fuzzy logic is used to generate dispatch plans.

Disk-Drive Spindle Motor Control

Seagate Technology [Tremaine 1994] has used fuzzy logic to control a spindle motor in a disk drive. The spin-up of the spindle motor from a dead stop using fuzzy integrated control shows less overshoot than with a classical PI controller.

Elevator Dispatch

The goal in this project is to efficiently dispatch elevator cars in a large building in order to minimize the individual waiting time for passengers. By applying fuzzy logic to this problem, Mitsubishi Electric achieved a 15 to 20 percent reduction in average waiting time and 30 to 40 percent reduction in long waits of 60 seconds or more. The variables used include when and where a hall button is pressed, hall congestion computed through a video image, and the position, speed and direction of each elevator car.

Environmental Monitoring

MCC spinoff Pavilion has used neural nets, chaos theory, and fuzzy logic to develop a barn-burning emissions monitor/predictor that chemical, oil, power, and paper companies are rapidly embracing [Washington Technology 1994]. Continuous Emission Monitoring (CEM) is typically done with hardware-based systems consisting of complex analyzers and sampling apparatus mounted in smokestacks. A single stack costs from $150,000 to $500,000, and requires $100,000 of annual maintenance. Because a typical chemical plant has 8 to 15 stacks, the total cost can be in the millions of dollars. Pavilion's Software CEM cuts these costs in half or more.

Heating and Cooling Control

Mitsubishi has developed a fuzzy system to control the rate of heat exchange, fan speed, and the direction of the louvers in each room of a building. The inputs to the system include room and wall temperature and rate of change in those temperatures. The system reduces heating and cooling times by a factor of five, improves temperature stability by a factor of two, and reduces the energy consumption by 24%.

Helicopter Control

Michio Sugeno at the Tokyo Institute of Technology has developed a helicopter that obeys the commands like "hover," "forward," "left," "up," and "land." He has used fuzzy logic to control the helicopter to achieve very good response and stability.

Process Control and Product Quality Control

A process is an operation of a setup that is intended to produce a product. Process control focuses on producing products according to some setpoints. Product quality control is different from process control. It focuses on generating correct setpoints for process control to produce good products. Fuzzy logic can be used in process control to generate control values based on the difference between the current values and setpoints of process variables. Fuzzy logic can also be used in product quality control to implement a product evaluation function which computes the "goodness" of a product. Once a product is evaluated, new setpoints for process control can be generated [Barnes 1996].

Semiconductor Manufacturing Process Automation

A state-of-the-art facility for manufacturing ICs in high volume typically costs several hundred million U.S. dollars. To offset this enormous investment, chip manufacturers must innovate to a greater degree in the fabrication processes in order to increase chip yields, reduce product cycle time, and maintain consistent levels of product quality and performance through Computer-Integrated Manufacturing (CIM) capabilities such as on-site process monitoring, process/equipment modeling, real-time closed-loop process control, and automated diagnosis of equipment malfunctions. Recently, neural network techniques have been applied to some of these problems [May 1994]. For example, the Georgia Institute of Technology has applied neural networks to model ion-assisted plasma etching, a process widely used in semiconductor manufacturing. In plasma etching, patterned layers of material are removed by reactive gases in an AC discharge. Input parameters are pressure, RF power, and gas composition. Process outputs are etch rate and etch uniformity. A neural network is used to establish a complex and non-linear relationship between the input parameters and the process outputs. Clearly, fuzzy logic can be used for the same purpose.

Sucker Rod Oil Pumping Control

Sucker rod pumping utilizes a motor at the surface to move a rod pump at the bottom of a well through steel tubes. A dynamometer measures the pump's load, and a position encoder senses its displacement. The load versus displacement curve reveals conditions of the pump. Excessive pumping or oil production rate produce distorted curves. The controller uses fuzzy logic to analyze the curve, and adjusts the pumping rate to compensate for any deviation from the ideal curve [Rocha et al. 1996].

Train Control

The problem is to achieve multiple goals such as running time, energy conservation, safety, comfort, and stopping accuracy. Hitatch has developed a predictive fuzzy logic system that evaluates the effects of several control commands to select the one that most satisfies all of the system's requirements. The result is a subway train in Sendai which can start and stop smoothly within 1.5 cm of a mark on the platform without passengers holding onto hand grips.

Transmission Control

An expert driver knows that he can brake a car on downhill grades by downshifting to a lower gear. The fuzzy logic transmission controller [Legg 1993] in every Saturn car with an automatic transmission uses 5 fuzzy rules to capture the expert's driving knowledge. It uses variables such as grade, speed, throttle position, brake-application time, brake application with high deceleration, and coasting with acceleration. Each rule involves some combination of these variables, such as, "if speed is low and grade is negative and brake application time is long, then downshift." The fuzzy controller evaluates the fuzzy rules four times each second to determine if it needs to shift gears.

Washing Machine

A fuzzy-logic-controlled washing machine made by Matsushita has a single button. The goal of the controller is to automatically adjust the amount of soap and water and washing time. The variables used are the size of the load of clothes, and the amount and type of dirt (e.g., soil or oil). An optical sensor is used to measure how much water is clouded, how long it takes for the clouding to reach saturation, and the level of saturation. From these measurements, it can determine the type and degree of dirt. These variables are then used in fuzzy rules.

Wind-Powered Generator

Using wind direction and speed as input, fuzzy logic is used by Klockner-Moeller to adjust rotor blade angle in order to manage mechanical stress due to fluctuating wind conditions, stabilize generated power, and minimize the slip between rotor and generator for best efficiency.

References

Barnes, R. [1996] "Hybrid-based PLC control predicts, optimizes product quality," *Control Engineering*, June 1996, pp.75-78.

Cox, E. [1993] "Adaptive fuzzy systems," *IEEE Spectrum*, February 1993, pp. 27-31.

Electronic Design [1994] "Neural network/fuzzy-logic technology enables intelligent and fast battery-charger circuit," *Electronic Design*, May 1, 1995, pp.38-40.

Jurgen, R. [1995] "The Electronic motorist," *IEEE Spectrum*, March 1995, pp. 37048.

Manji, J.F. [1995] "Fuzzy logic creates new applications," *Managing Automation*, August 1995, pp. 49-51.

May, G.S. [1994] "Manufacturing ICs the neural way," *IEEE Spectrum*, September 1994, pp. 47-51.

Legg, G. [1993] "Transmission's fuzzy logic keeps you on track," *EDN*, December 23, 1993, pp. 60-63.

Rocha, A.F., Morooka, C.K., and Alegre, L. [1996] "Smart oil recovery," *IEEE Spectrum*, July 1996, pp. 48-51.

Tremaine, B.P. [1994] "Weigh the benifits of fuzzy-logic vs classical control in a disk-drive spindle," *EDN*, July 7, 1994, pp. 137-144.

Vieira, P., and Gomide, F. [1996] "Computer-aided train dispatch," *IEEE Spectrum*, July 1996, pp.51-53.

Washington Technology [1994] "A warm fuzzy for environmental monitoring," *Washinton Technology*, March 24, 1994.

Williams, T. [1991] "Fuzzy logic simplifies complex control problems," *Computer Design*, March 1, 1991, pp. 90-99.

Appendix G   Some Applications In Pattern Recognition

Coronary Artery Stenosis Diagnosis

Scintigraphic images of a patient's heart from different views are
used to predict which parts of main arteries have stenosis
(narrowing). Regions of the heart with less-than-normal blood flow
are said to have a perfusion defect. A scintigraphic image is divided
into 10 regions, and the number of pixels in each region is counted.
About 100 patients' data are used to train fuzzy rules that relate the
number of pixels to the degree of perfusion defect [Cios et al. 1991].

Credit Card Fraud Detection

It is estimated that the total credit card fraud loss in the U.S. runs
over a billion dollars a year. XTec Inc has developed a system
[Corbin 1994] that can recognize whether a card is valid or not.
Every magnetic stripe-based card has unique and can-not-be-copied-
or-duplicated "jitters" that can be used as a signature of the card.
Every time a credit card is read, its signature is compared with the
stored signature through the use of fuzzy logic. It has demonstrated
that the system can achieve very high level of credit card security.

DC Motor Short Circuit Diagnosis

A new DC motor is tested by first measuring its coil resistance,
operating temperature, and noise, and then classified by fuzzy rules
for whether there is a short circuit in the winding or not
[Angstenerger and Weber 1995].

Handwriting Character Recognition

It is easy to start a handwriting character recognition project on a PC
platform running the Microsoft Windows operating system and
using a digitizer pad for the user handwriting input. The input to the
handwriting character recognizer is a sequence of points captured
from the operating system through the digitizer pad. The recognizer
will perform normalization, feature extraction, matching, and

classification. Fuzzy logic can be used in some/all of these operations. An example of a fuzzy logic handwriting character recognition project is given in [Auzas 1994].

Fast Image Delivery Over Internet

An image is divided into several layers, and each layer is encoded by different compression algorithms. The Johnson Grace Company (Newport Beach, CA, Phone 714-759-0700) has used fuzzy logic to first assess the general character of an image, and then choose an optimal sequence of combinational codecs to compress the layers of the image [Doherty 1995]. For example, the first two layers of an image may be sub-band encoded and decoded, while the final detailed layers may be compressed via Vector Quantization or other imaging technologies. The trick is recognizing which approaches work best for which image types. The first layer can be delivered very quickly using a low bandwidth modem over the Internet so that a Web browser can get enough of an idea of the image's subject content to decide whether to keep downloading the remainder or to move on to another image page.

Medical Image Analysis and Diagnosis

Each year any hospital or medical center takes thousands and thousands of medical images such as X-ray, PAP smear images, etc. The work load of handling these images is overwhelming. Fuzzy logic can be used to solve some of the medical image analysis and diagnosis problems.

Oil Drilling Assistant

An expert system assists drilling engineers by identifying abnormalities and advising them on the appropriate action to take in offshore oil drilling. Many accidents are presaged by variations in such parameters as torque and rotation of the drilling column, and pressure in the space around the column. These data are sampled constantly. By using fuzzy logic, a system has been built to construct a consistent database on normal and abnormal drilling operations, and predicts and diagnoses possible abnormalities to provide adequate backup to maintenance and repair [Rocha et al. 1996].

Oil Production Process Automation

The function of a process plant is to receive input from many wells in a field; separate oil, gas, and water; and deliver the produced oil and gas. Using pressure sensors that monitor the gas lift process, and flow sensors that indicate the blend of oil and gas produced, a fuzzy-logic-based system has been built to help the plant operators decide whether the process must be rerouted (excess gas burned so as to reduce output flow), or whether the plant must be shut down if faced with abnormal production, operation, or delivery conditions. Because of this automation, the system has reduced plant shutdown frequency by 80 percent [Rocha et al. 1996].

Speech Recognition

It is easy to start a speech recognition project on a PC platform running the Microsoft Windows operating system and using a sound/voice card for the user voice input. The input to the speech recognizer is a digital representation of a voice waveform captured from the operating system through the sound/voice card. The recognizer will perform segmentation, digital signal processing such as filtering and Fast Fourier Transformation (FFT), feature extraction, matching, and classification. Fuzzy logic can be used in some/all of these operations. An example of a fuzzy logic speech recognition project is given in [Fennich 1994].

Tile Crack Detection

Tiles are manufactured as follows: First, raw material is pressed into the correct form. Second, the surfaces of the tiles are brushed, after which a galze is applied. Finally, the tiles are burnt in a furnace. During this process, cracks which are not visible from the outside may occur inside a tile. If the tile is struck with a hammer, one can tell if it is good or bad on the basis of the sound emitted by the struck tile. This disgnosis method is automated by using fuzzy logic [Angstenerger and Weber 1995].

<u>Time to Change Oil?</u>

The University of Dayton and Wright Laboratory at Wright-Patterson Air Force Base have developed an electronic probe that tells users when it's time to change transmission oil in cars or cooking oil in deep-fat fryers. Normally, oil contains the antioxidant additive to keep it from degrading too fast. The probe measures the remaining of the antioxidant in oil and tells if it's time to change oil. This project may not use fuzzy logic, but it is a good practical problem for fuzzy logic to tackle.

References

Angstenerger, J., and Weber, R. [1995] "Quality control using fuzzy techniques and neural networks," *Proceedings of Fuzzy Logic'95*, Computer Design, PennWell Publishing Company, Ten Tara Blvd, Nashua, NH 03062-2801.

Auzas, E. [1994] "Handwriting letter recognition using fuzzy methods," *Fuzzy Logic Applications Handbook*, Order Number 272589-002, Intel Literature Sales, P.O. Box 7641, Mt. Prospect, IL 60056-7641, USA, Tel. 800-548-4725.

Cios, K.J., Shin, I., and Goodenday, L.S. [1991] "Using fuzzy sets to diagnose coronary artery stenosis," *IEEE Computer*, March 1991, pp. 57-63.

Corbin, J. [1994] "A fuzzy-logic-based financial transaction system," *Embedded Systems Programming*, December 1994, pp. 24-29.

Doherty, R. [1995] "Speed to screen imaging success: Remaking low bit-rate online image delivery at Johnson Grace," *Advanced Imaging*, October 1995, pp. 33-36.

Fennich, M. [1994] "Voice input calculator using fuzzy logic,"
    Fuzzy Logic Applications Handbook, Order
    Number 272589-002, Intel Literature Sales, P.O. Box 7641,
    Mt. Prospect, IL 60056-7641, USA, Tel. 800-548-4725.

Rocha, A.F., Morooka, C.K., and Alegre, L. [1996] "Smart oil
    recovery," *IEEE Spectrum*, July 1996, pp.48-51.

Appendix H.   LEADTOOLS DLL Functions

Function	Description
L_AccessBitmap	Provides exclusive access to a bitmap.
L_AddBitmapNoise	Adds random pixels to a bitmap.
L_AllocateBitmap	Allocates storage to hold an image.
L_AverageFilterBitmap	Averages pixel colors.
L_BinaryFilterBitmap	Imposes a binary filter on a bitmap.
L_ChangeBitmapContrast	Changes a bitmap's contrast.
L_ChangeBitmapHeight	Changes the allocated height of a bitmap.
L_ChangeBitmapHue	Changes the hue of colors in a bitmap.
L_ChangeBitmapIntensity	Changes the intensity in a bitmap.
L_ChangeBitmapSaturation	Changes the saturation of colors in a bitmap.
L_ChangeFromDDB	Changes a DDB bitmap to a LEAD bitmap.
L_ChangeFromDIB	Changes a DIB bitmap to a LEAD bitmap.
L_ChangeToDDB	Changes a LEAD bitmap to a DDB bitmap.
L_ChangeToDIB	Changes a LEAD bitmap to a DIB bitmap.
L_ClearBitmap	Sets all bits to 0 in a bitmap.
L_ClipboardReady	Does the clipboard contain a bitmap?
L_ColorMergeBitmap	Merges grayscale bitmaps to a color bitmap.
L_ColorResBitmap	Converts a bitmap from a resolution to another.
L_ColorSeparateBitmap	Slides a color bitmap into grayscale bitmaps.
L_CombineBitmap	Combines two bitmaps.
L_CompressBitmapWithStamp	Compresses a bitmap to a thumbnail image.
L_CompressBuffer	Does buffer-to-buffer JPEG or CMP compression.
L_CompressData	Compresses data in a buffer.
L_ConvertBuffer	Converts data in a buffer to an image resolution.
L_ConvertColorSpace	Converts from one color space model to another.
L_ConvertFromDDB	Converts a DDB bitmap to a LEAD bitmap.
L_ConvertFromDIB	Converts a DIB bitmap to a LEAD bitmap.
L_ConvertToDDB	Converts a LEAD bitmap to a DDB bitmap.
L_CopyBitmap	Copies a bitmap.
L_CopyBitmapData	Copies image data from a bitmap.
L_CopyBitmapHandle	Copies one bitmap handle to another.
L_CopyBitmapRect	Copies a portion of a bitmap into another bitmap.
L_CopyFromClipboard	Copies image data from the clipboard.
L_CopyToClipboard	Copies raster image data to the clipboard.
L_CopyToClipboardExt	Copies rsater or RGB image data to the clipboard.
L_CreateBitmap	Initializes and allocates a bitmap.
L_CreateLeadDC	Uses a bitmap to create a device context.
L_CreatePaintPalette	Returns a palette handle.
L_CreateUserMatchTable	Creates a table for speedy color conversion.
L_DecompressBitmapMemory	Decompresses a file in memory to a bitmap.
L_DecompressData	Notifies system to decompress the data in a buffer.

L_DecompressMemory	Decompresses a file in memory to a buffer.
L_DefaultDithering	Specifies the default dithering method.
L-DeskewBitmap	Straightens a bitmap.
L_DespeckleBitmap	Removes speckles from a bitmap.
L_DitherLine	Dithers a line in an input buffer.
L_DupPalette	Duplicates a Windows palette.
L_EmbossBitmap	Applies an emboss effect to a bitmap.
L_EndCompressBuffer	Clears buffers allocated by compression engine.
L_EndCompressData	Clears buffers allocated by lossless comp. engine.
L_FileConvert	Converts a file format to another.
L_FileInfo	Gets information about a file.
L_FileInfoMemory	Loads file info. in memory into a FILEINFO struc.
L_FillBitmap	Fills a bitmap with a specified color.
L_FlipBitmap	Flips a bitmap from top to buttom.
L_FreeBitmap	Frees storage allocated for a bitmap.
L_FreeUserMatchTable	Frees a table used for speed conversion.
L_GammaCorrectBitmap	Changes gamma constant to adjust color intensities.
L_GetBitmapColors	Loads colors from a bitmap's palette.
L_GetBitmapHistogram	Creates an intensity level histogram for a bitmap.
L_GetBitmapRow	Retrieves a row from a bitmap.
L_GetBitmapRowCol	Retrieves data from a bitmap.
L_GetComment	Gets a current field to be saved as a comment.
L_GetCompressFileStamp	Reads a thumbnail stored in a compressed file.
L_GetDisplayMode	Gets the painting control flags.
L_GetFixedPalette	Gets the colors of the fixed palette.
L_GetPCDResolution	Gets a PhotoCD file's resolutions.
L_GetPixelColor	Gets the RGB color values of a pixel.
L_GrayScaleBitmap	Converts a bitmap to an 8-bit gray scale bitmap.
L_HalftoneBitmap	Converts a bitmap to a halftoned bitmap.
L_HalftoneBitmapExt	Converts to a halftoned bitmap with a rotation.
L_HistoContrastBitmap	Changes the contrast of a bitmap based on histo.
L_HistoEqualizeBitmap	Linearizes the num. of pixels per grap level.
L_InitBitmap	Initializes the fields in a bitmap handle.
L_IntensityDetectBitmap	Filters a bitmap to detect colors in a range.
L_InvertBitmap	Inverts the colors in a bitmap.
L_LoadBitmap	Loads an image file into a bitmap.
L_LoadBitmapMemory	Loads an image file from memory into a bitmap.
L_LoadFile	Loads a file.
L_LoadFileOffset	Loads an image in a file.
L_LoadMemory	Loads a file from memory.
L_MedianFilterBitmap	Changes the color of each pixel to the median color.
L_MosaicBitmap	Imposes a mosaic effect on a bitmap.
L_PaintDC	Displays an image to any device context.
L_PaintDCBuffer	Paints image into a device context from a buffer.
L_PaintDCEffect	Applies an effect when painting to a screen.
L_PosterizeBitmap	Imposes a poster effect on a bitmap.
L_PrintBitmap	Prints a bitmap.

L_PrintBitmapExt	Prints a bitmap to a specified device.
L_PrintBitmapFast	Prints a bitmap to a specified device.
L_PutBitmapColors	Updates the bitmap handle's palette.
L_PutBitmapRow	Copies a row from an image buffer to a bitmap.
L_PutBitmapRowCol	Copies data from a buffer to a bitmap.
L_PutPixelColor	Changes RGB the color value of a pixel.
L_ReadFileComment	Gets a comment field from a TIFF file header.
L_RedirectIO	Redirects I/O functions for opening, reading, etc.
L_ReleaseBitmap	Releases memory back to Windows.
L_RemapBitmapIntensity	Changes a bitmap's intensity values.
L_ResampleBitmap	Resizes a bitmap,using interpolation and averaging.
L_Resize	Resizes a buffer.
L_ResizeBitmap	Resizes the image from a bitmap.
L_ReverseBitmap	Reverses a bitmap from left to right.
L_RotateBitmap	Rotates a bitmap by certain degrees.
L_RotateBitmapFine	Rotates a bitmap by certain hundredths of degrees.
L_SaveBitmap	Saves an image in a bitmap to a file.
L_SaveBitmapMemory	Saves a bitmap to a file in memory.
L_SaveFile	Creates a file and save input data into the file.
L_SaveFileOffset	Saves a bitmap to a file with an offset.
L_ScreenCaptureBitmap	Loads a bitmap from a rectangle in a DC.
L_SetComment	Saves a field as a comment in a TIFF file header.
L_SetDisplayMode	Sets flags that control painting operations.
L_SetLoadInfoCallback	Specifies a callback for handling input data.
L_SetPCDResolution	Sets the resolution for a PhotoCD file.
L_SetStatusCallBack	Specifies a callback for updating a status bar.
L_SetUserMatchTable	Selects a table for speedy conversion.
L_SharpenBitmap	Changes the sharpness of the image in a bitmap.
L_ShearBitmap	Moves the corners of a bitmap.
L_SizeBitmap	Resizes a bitmap to a new width and height.
L_SpatialFilterBitmap	Imposes a spatial filter on a bitmap.
L_StartCompressBuffer	Initializes the buffered compression engine.
L_StartCompressData	Initializes the lossless compression process.
L_StartDecompressData	Initializes the lossless decompression process.
L_StartDithering	Initializes the buffered dithering of a bitmap.
L_StartResize	Sets up information for the L_Resize function.
L_StopDithering	Clears buffers allocated by L_StartDithering.
L_StopResize	Clears buffers allocated by L_StartResize.
L_StretchBitmapIntensity	Increases the contrast in an image.
L_TwainAcquire	Loads a bitmap from a TWAIN device.
L_TwainAcquireExt	Loads bitmaps from multipage scanning.
L_TwainEnumSources	Finds the name of each available TWAIN source.
L_TwainSelect	Selects a TWAIN source for scanning.
L_TwainSetProps	Sets TWAIN session properties.
L_UnderlayBitmap	Combines two bitmaps to underlay one on another.
L_VersionInfo	Loads LEADTOOLS information into a structure.

Appendix I.   GLIDE 2.1 Library Functions

<u>Image Acquisition (Frame Grabber Control)</u>

Single frame acquisition
Frame averaging up to 256 frames
Live video enable/disable
Video input channel selection
Hardware gain, offset, and reference adjustment
Input look-up table selection and loading
External or internal sync source selection
External trigger
Frame grabber setup and status

<u>Image Analysis and Measurement</u>

Particle analysis
Selection of which measurements are reported
Mean gray value, Area of object, Total area, Hole area, Hole ratio, Ratio of square
    root of perimeter to total, Area, Number of holes in object, Min and max value
    of X and Y, X pixel coordinate corresponding to Y value, Y pixel coordinate
    corresponding to X value, Perimeter, Length of perimeter along X or Y axis,
    First or second moments of area in X,Y, or X and Y, X,Y center of gravity,
    Major o minor axis, Axis ratio, Angle between horizontal and major axis,
    Min or max radius from center of area to perimeter, Angle of in or max radius,
    Difference between angles of min and max radii, Average radius, Ratio of min
    to max radius, Ratio of width to length, Extend of object along X or Y axis,
    Bounding box area, Length or width of bounding box, Ratio of area of object
    to bounding box area, Distance from coordinate origin to center of object,
    Roundness (circularity), Symmetry along major or minor axis
Return of number of objects found that meet the specified size and intensity
    threshold settings, Size range selection to determine which objects are included
    and which are ignored
Grayscale threshold selection for desired objetcs to determine which are included
    and which are ignored, Highlighting of selected objects on the display
Particle class definition and classification
Intensity measurements, Intensity measurement along a specified line, Histogram
    in a rectangular region, Intensity measurement at a point, Coordinate positions
    along a line

<u>Image Processing</u>

Enhancement Filters: Sobel radient, Arithmetic mean, Median filter with
    user-defined shape, Cross gradient, Roberts gradient, Horizontal gradient,
    Vertical gradient, Diamond gradient, Left diagonal gradient, Right diagonal

gradient, Image sharpening (Laplacian), Selection of filter gain value (for
normalization), Selection of offset filter value (for normalization),
User-defined with kernels of any size and shape

Morphological Filters: Dilation, Erosion, Opening, Closing, Setting of the
number of iterations, User-defined with structuring elements of any size and
shape

Arithmetic and Logical Operations: Arithmetic add, subtract, multiply, divide,
DIF (between two buffers), Logical AND, OR, XOR, NOT (between two
buffers), Arithmetic add, subtract, multiply, divide (between a buffer and
a constant)

Geometric Transforms: User-defined geometric transform (using a transform
matrix)

Frequency Processing: FFTs and inverse FFTs, Frequency spectrum editing (pass
or reject part of spectrum)

Linear transforms (input LUT processing)

Display

Buffer selection for display
Zoom factor selection
Pan and scroll control
Straight line, free form, and rectangular graphics
Bitmap rendering to display buffer
Display enable/disable
Copying pixel data from a system buffer to onboard display buffer
Grphic object display refresh manipulation
Display characteristics and status
False coloring (overlay LUT manipulation)

Image File I/O

Save or load images in TIFF, DT-IRIS, or PCX format

Buffer Manipulation

Buffer allocation/deallocation
Put pixel values (rectangle, line, or single pixel) from location (X,Y) in a buffer
into local memory
Put pixel values from local memory into a buffer (rectangle, line, or single pixel)
starting at location (X,Y)
Copy from one buffer to another
Buffer status

INDEX

A

A/D converter, 47-48
Air pollution category, 91
Analog input, 47-48
Analog output, 48-49
Analysis hardware, 50
ANSWER table, 143-144
Arithmetic expression, 24-25
Automatic transmission control, 217

B

Bandpass filter, 97-99
Battery-charger control, 217
Block matching method for image segmentation, 118-120

C

Centroid method, 7
Comment statement, 9-10, 23
Comparison across dimensions, 145-149
Complex query, 145-149
Computer-aided train dispatch, 217
Constant, 24
Contact classifiction problem, 108
Content-based retrieval, 151-152
Control decision, 1
Control system, 61-83, 217-222
Coronary artery stenosis diagnosis, 223
Counter, 49
Credit card fraud detection, 223

M

Machine learning, 183-195
Machine tool breakage detection, 105-107
Machine training, 183-195
Machine vision, 124-127
Mathematical model, 61
Medical image analysis and diagnosis, 224
Membership function, 2-3, 11, 27-29
Membership package statement, 9-12, 30-33
Multiple performance criterion, 193-195

N

NICEL language, 9, 23-43, 182
NICEL compiler, 12, 38

O

OCX, 113-116
Oil-change detection, 226
Oil drilling assistant, 224
Oil production process automation, 225
Operator, 24
Optimization problem, 183
Output, 1, 48-49
Overall system performance criterion, 193-195
Overshoot, 67-68

P

Pattern classification, 87-108, 223-227
Pattern discovery, 159-160, 168
Pattern recognition, 87-108, 167-172, 189-192, 223-227
Performance criterion, 193-195
Piecewise linear function, 178-179
Ping-pong ball controller, 65-66
Pixel, 113

W

Z